CIRCLE OF PEACE
Reflections on the Bahá'í Teachings

Books in this series:

Circle of Unity: Bahá'í Approaches to Current Social Issues
Circle of Peace: Reflections on the Bahá'í Teachings

CIRCLE OF PEACE

Reflections on the Bahá'í Teachings

Edited by Anthony A. Lee

Kalimát Press
Los Angeles

First Edition

Copyright © 1985 by Kalimát Press
All Rights Reserved

Manufactured in the United States of America

"What About the Russians?"
Copyright © 1985 by Bradley Pokorny

Library of Congress Cataloging in Publication Data

Main entry under title:
Circle of peace: reflections on the Bahá'í teachings.
Contents: Bahá'ís and the peace movement / by Richard Hollinger—World peace / by Robert T. Phillips—The global agenda / by Charles O. Lerche [etc.]
Includes bibliographies.
1. Bahai Faith—Doctrines—Addresses, essays, lectures. 2. Peace—Religious aspects—Bahai Faith—Addresses, essays, lectures. I. Lee, Anthony A., 1947- .
BP370.C55 1986   297'.892   85-23287
ISBN 0-933770-48-0

To
my dearest wife
FLOR
and to
FAIZI and TARAZ
and to all those yet unborn
whom I hope will live to see a world
at peace

CONTENTS

Introduction *by Anthony A. Lee* ix

Bahá'ís and American Peace Movements
Richard Hollinger 3

World Peace: The Dream in Daylight
Robert T. Phillips 21

The Global Agenda
Charles O. Lerche 41

Human Rights and World Peace
Tahmineh Roshanian 61

Peace Groups and the Global Pact
Rouha Rose 79

Bringing In The Dawn: Women and Peace
Susan Brill 99

Bahá'í Youth in the Peace Movement
Karin Ryan Barnes 125

Continued

A Bahá'í Goes to War
David Langness 145

What About The Russians?
Brad Pokorny 185

Biographical Notes 213

Introduction

THE TEACHING OF PEACE can, of course, be found in all the world's great faiths. But in no religion is the issue of peace among nations more central to the concerns and convictions of the believers than in the Bahá'í Faith. Passage after passage in the Writings of Bahá'u'lláh, its Prophet and Founder, speak directly to this question. Indeed, the future establishment of the Most Great Peace—the unification of all peoples and nations of the world—Bahá'u'lláh established as the goal and crowning achievement of His mission.

When Professor E. G. Browne of Cambridge University visited Him in Palestine in 1890, during the last years of His life, Bahá'u'lláh addressed His first words to the theme of peace and unity. Browne records Him saying:

> *That all nations should become one in faith and all men as brothers; that the bonds of affection and unity between the sons of men should be strengthened; that diversity of religion should cease, and differences of race be annulled—what harm is there in this? . . . Yet so it shall be; these fruitless strifes, these ruinous wars shall pass away, and the "Most Great Peace" shall come. . . . Do not you in Europe need this also? Is not this that which Christ foretold? . . . Yet do we see your kings and rulers lavishing their treasures more freely on*

> *means for the destruction of the human race than on that which would conduce to the happiness of mankind. . . . These strifes and this bloodshed and discord must cease, and all men be as one kindred and one family. . . . Let not a man glory in this, that he loves his country; let him rather glory in this, that he loves his kind. . . ."* (*A Traveller's Narrative*, p. xl)

The Bahá'í focus on world peace was intensified by 'Abdu'l-Bahá, the eldest son of Bahá'u'lláh, who was appointed by his Father as His successor and who was the head of the Bahá'í Faith from 1892 until his own passing in 1921. During his travels in Europe and America (1911–1912), 'Abdu'l-Bahá made the issue of international peace a major theme of his public addresses. Repeatedly he warned of the dangers of war and outlined the moral and social reforms that are the prerequisites of any universal and lasting peace.

His counsels unheeded, 'Abdu'l-Bahá returned to the Holy Land, and Europe plunged into World War I. After witnessing that catastrophe, he wrote:

> *This recent war has proved to the world and the people that war is destruction while universal peace is construction; war is death while peace is life; war is rapacity and bloodthirstiness while peace is beneficence and humaneness; war is an appurtenance of the world of nature while peace is of the foundation of the religion of God; war is darkness upon darkness while peace is heavenly light; war is the destroyer of the edifice of mankind while peace is the everlasting life of the world of humanity; war is like a devouring wolf while peace is like the angels of heaven; war is the struggle for existence while peace is mutual aid and co-operation among the peoples of the world and the cause of the good-pleasure of the True One in the heavenly realm.*
>
> *There is not one soul whose conscience does not testify that*

in this day there is no more important matter in the world than that of universal peace. (*Waging Peace*, p. 11)

A large part of the writings of Shoghi Effendi, Guardian of the Bahá'í Faith from 1921 to 1957, address the question of world order and international peace. He decried the impotence of statesmanship to achieve these goals and dedicated his life to the organization of the Bahá'í community around the world as a model and workshop for the coming new world civilization.

More recently, the Universal House of Justice, now the highest authority in the Bahá'í religion, distributed a letter to world leaders urging them to convene an international convocation for the purpose of deliberating on the establishment of permanent world peace. This peace statement, addressed to "the peoples of the world," acknowledges the central position that the teaching of world peace occupies in the consciousness of the Bahá'í community.

Notwithstanding this urgent concern, it would, of course, be a mistake to regard the Bahá'í Faith as a peace society. Bahá'ís regard their faith as a world religion which must influence all aspects of human life—individual and collective. Furthermore, the Bahá'í writings maintain that the international peace they seek will finally be achieved through the work of organizations, and by the decisions of governments, *outside* the Bahá'í community, and not through any direct actions on the part of the Bahá'í Faith. Bahá'ís refer to this as the Lesser Peace—a cessation of war and a unity among nations to be established by world leaders on the basis of political necessity, motivated by fear and practical advantage. This Bahá'ís contrast with a more distant Most Great Peace —the spiritual as well as political unity of mankind, raised on moral foundations, a peace that will bring depth, meaning, and irrevocable permanence to the political cease-fire.

A letter written on behalf of the Guardian to an individual Bahá'í reads:

With reference to the question you have asked concerning the time and means through which the Lesser and Most Great Peace, referred to by Bahá'u'lláh will be established. . . . Your view that the Lesser Peace will come about through the political efforts of the States and Nations of the world and independently of any direct Bahá'í plan or effort . . . —your view of this subject is quite correct, and in full accord with the pronouncements of the Guardian . . . (Dated March 14, 1939. *Lights of Guidance*, p. 323)

Therefore, Bahá'ís must feel a duty to work with peace organizations outside the range of their religion to bring about the Lesser Peace so vital to the survival of humanity. Realizing that no efforts within the Bahá'í community can win this longed-for goal, they associate and affiliate when possible— as individuals and collectively—with peace groups working to eliminate the curse of war from human history. It is altogether appropriate that they should do so. Bahá'u'lláh Himself, in His "Tablet of the World," addressed the elected representatives of the Bahá'í community, saying:

It is incumbent upon the ministers of the House of Justice to promote the Lesser Peace so that the people of the earth may be relieved from the burden of exorbitant expenditures. This matter is imperative and absolutely essential, inasmuch as hostilities and conflict lie at the root of affliction and calamity. (Tablets of Bahá'u'lláh, p. 89)

Moreover, even before his visit to America 'Abdu'l-Bahá had urged Bahá'ís to become involved in peace societies:

Truly I say many societies are organized in America for the promotion of the thought of peace and universal brotherhood. That country has preceded all the rest in this respect. But all these peace societies organized in the countries of the West, whose aim is the oneness of the realm of humanity, consist of explanations and theories on this subject; but the Bahá'ís have engraved this matter on the page of this world with their own blood. Through the power of the Word of God they have unfurled the banner of the oneness of the kingdom of humanity upon the apex of the world with deeds and actions; and through the bounty of Bahá'u'lláh they have spread the proclamation of the brotherhood of man and the universal equality among the people of the East and the West. Herein consists the difference.

. . . Notwithstanding this, the Bahá'ís must associate and become members of these peace societies, so that they may awaken them to the realization that this great cause of universal peace cannot be established and maintained except through the power of God . . . (Waging Peace, pp. 33–34)

The Guardian of the Bahá'í Faith also insisted on the need for Bahá'ís to lend their assistance to the different movements working for peace and for other progressive goals. For example, on his behalf his secretary wrote to a Bahá'í in Canada:

The Cause will not attain its aim and order in the great reign of peace unless its principles are put into practice. We have to assist the different movements which have progressive ideas and are striving for an aim similar to ours.

We have to help every such society even if it is merely to abolish the prejudice and ill feeling which prevails . . . Provided always that we do not entangle the Cause in political issues and party affiliations. (*Bahá'í News*, No. 10, February 1926, p. 7)

THE UNITED NATIONS proclamation of 1986 as the International Year of Peace marked a turning point in the attitudes and actions of Bahá'ís toward the worldwide peace movement. In response to this call, the Universal House of Justice urged all local and national Bahá'í communities to sponsor a variety of peace-related activities that might call the attention of the people of the world to this vital issue. (Letter of January 23, 1985, *Bahá'í News*, No. 648, March 1985, p. 1) Bahá'ís were encouraged to plan events both as Bahá'í communities and in concert with their fellow workers for peace in other organizations.

Such an emphasis on peace activities, fostered from the World Center of the Faith, catapulted the issue of international peace to the top of the Bahá'í agenda. Local Bahá'í groups began initiating contact with peace organizations on an unprecedented scale—planning conferences, lectures, seminars, awards presentations, contests, and demonstrations. Their efforts were fired by the lengthy statement summarizing the Bahá'í teachings on peace and world unity released by the House of Justice late in 1985. This statement has become the new basis of Bahá'í thought and action on this issue.

Nonetheless, the recent high levels of peace advocacy in the Bahá'í community are still tentative and unsure. Bahá'ís are yet doubtful about how best to approach their new task, especially about how to relate to other organizations committed to the same goal but through different means.

I BELIEVE, however, that this hesitancy will be short lived. As Bahá'ís become more involved in the peace movement, as they come into closer contact with peace organizations, and build relationships with other peace workers, they will discover that the Bahá'í community has much to offer. The Bahá'í sacred writings and the experience that Bahá'ís have gained while building a unified world community provide profound insights into the nature of the struggle for peace. They will find the peace movement today sadly fragmented and directionless and, in its organized form at least, often frustratingly shallow and naive.

The Universal House of Justice in its statement on peace promised the peoples of the world that "if the Bahá'í experience can contribute in whatever measure to reinforcing hope in the unity of the human race, we are happy to offer it. . . . '' That experience—long, deep, committed, international as it is—belongs not just to the Bahá'ís, but to mankind as a whole. We must be willing to share it with all those who wish to learn from its successes and failures. Let us examine a few of the insights into the nature of world peace that Bahá'ís might offer to the movement:

A Culture of Peace. Bahá'ís understand that peace cannot be established in a vacuum, or among nations that are actively opposed to it in word or deed. As 'Abdu'l-Bahá explained, peace requires certain social, cultural, economic, and moral foundations if it is to be achieved. 'Abdu'l-Bahá proclaimed these foundations as the Bahá'í Peace Program, but they are more commonly known to Bahá'ís as the "twelve principles" of their Faith. These are:

1. The oneness of mankind,
2. The independent investigation of truth,
3. The elimination of prejudice of all kinds—racial, cultural, national, religious, etc.,
4. The equality of men and women,
5. Agreement between science and religion,
6. The common foundation of all religions,
7. Religion must be the cause of harmony and unity,
8. A spiritual solution to the economic problem,
9. Universal education,
10. A universal auxiliary language,
11. An international tribunal,
12. International peace.

Clearly, from a Bahá'í point of view, the pursuit of peace cannot be a narrow activity directed toward a single goal. Rather, the establishment of peace will require a complex of activities directed toward multiple issues. The goal of this work is not simply the cessation of war, but the growth and development of a culture of peace that will support a new international order.

Peace is an active process, not a passive condition. For Bahá'ís, the struggle for peace is not just a matter of being against war. It is the building of a new kind of society that makes peace possible. The only way to eliminate war is to *wage peace*. Otherwise, there are colossal social forces at work that push us continually toward war—not only military and industrial networks, political establishments, and centuries of history, but more abstractly ignorance, prejudice, economic disparity, and the decline of religion.

Making the connection between such basic Bahá'í principles as the unity of mankind and the peace movement's quest for world peace may not be as easy as it would seem. Not long ago I served on an interreligious peace committee as the Bahá'í representative. The committee's major activity for the year was to sponsor a high school essay contest on the theme of world peace. It was a worthy project, and it met with a good deal of success. Hundreds of students submitted essays, and so were challenged to think more deeply about the vital questions of peace and disarmament. The ten finalists were invited to an awards banquet where the winners were to be announced. A number of Bahá'ís were present.

The banquet was well attended—some two hundred students, parents, teachers, and workers for peace came. The speakers were impressive. But, as we looked around the room, the Bahá'ís were stunned and embarrassed to discover that everyone in the room was white, except for a few of us.

At the next meeting of the interreligious committee, I raised the question cautiously. Noting that Bahá'ís believe in building a culture of peace (a goal that all approved of), I explained that the most important element of that culture is the oneness of mankind, that this included the elimination of all kinds of prejudices, as well as interracial and intercultural cooperation. (Again, all agreed.) Then I noted that everyone at the banquet had been white.

The committee members stared at me blankly.

I went on to say that this was surely an oversight, but that we must avoid a repeat in the future. Perhaps we could invite some black churches to send representatives to the committee. (Still no response.) How could we, after all, expect to be taken seriously in our commitment to international peace if we did not demonstrate at least interracial unity in our meetings.

Silence. After a short while, someone politely changed the subject.

These were devoted workers for peace, men and women with whom I had worked, whom I know had sweated and sacrificed to bring an end to war. But they simply saw no relationship between these efforts and the need to insure interracial fellowship in their meetings.

Means and Ends. As Bahá'ís work in the peace movement, they will find that the question of methods always arises. What can we *do* to bring about peace? Occasionally, a Bahá'í may find himself uncomfortable with a course of action that is partisan and political, illegal, abrasive, morally questionable, or simply impolite. At such a point, one might be able to contribute the insight that, from a Bahá'í point of view, there can be no separation made between means and ends.

The ends, in fact, are simply means carried out to their ultimate conclusions.

The Role of Women: Another insight that Bahá'ís can bring to the peace movement is the understanding that women have a primary role to play in the establishment of world peace. Women through history have developed and cultivated certain feminine qualities and behaviors that the human race now finds vital to its survival. Gentleness, patience, cooperation, acceptance, nurturance, nonviolence—these are traditionally female traits. Moreover, certain survival skills, such as the sense to retreat when appropriate, the clever avoidance of confrontation, the art of persuasion, are taught and practiced in women's culture.

Men must be willing to learn these skills and apply them

to society in such a way that male and female characteristics will be more balanced. Women must take the initiative to demand an end to war, and to offer feminine insights into how to build a world that will be free of it.

The Power of Faith. Peace movements, especially those that have appeared in Europe and America, have been notoriously and tragically short-lived. Popular feeling for creating international peace has repeatedly been cut short by war, or simply exhausted and disillusioned by the realization that the task is an arduous one.

Today there is a rush of hope that we can quickly ban nuclear weapons, reverse the arms race, or eliminate war altogether. But such goals will not be accomplished this year—possibly they will not be accomplished in our lifetimes, and possibly not in our children's lifetimes. Does the present peace movement command the mature commitment to carry us through the long haul? to sustain perhaps a generation of struggle? perhaps two generations? perhaps more?

Possibly it is only religious faith that can sustain such long-term commitment. Bahá'ís, finding international peace as a basic and central tenet of their religion, will remain active workers for peace for as long as necessary.

A Mature Vision. Most peace groups, though they struggle against the prospect of war, have no clear idea of the kind of peaceful world they want to see replace it. Most admit that they have no mature vision of a better world, only a keen sense (and an accurate one) of the evils that plague us now. The Bahá'í Faith, with its principles of economic justice, world federalism, social equality, and spiritual reawakening can offer a pattern for a future society that is full and elaborate. Bahá'ís are not preoccupied with gloom and doom, nor do we offer only vague hopes, pious ideals, and glittering generalities.

ALL THIS DOES NOT SUGGEST that Bahá'ís have all the answers. Nor can we consider ourselves superior, even in our vision, to other groups that work for peace. As explained above, Bahá'ís acknowledge openly that peace groups outside of the Faith, with their real and vast experience in the world, have *more* to contribute to the coming Lesser Peace than we do. We are yet new to the struggle, a struggle that will eventually be won by others.

The point is only that Bahá'ís may have a role to play in that struggle—and perhaps a significant one—if we will play it. As newcomers to the peace movement, we must be prepared to learn more than we teach. We must expect that we will confront new issues, unexpected problems and difficulties. We must be prepared to develop new strategies, new ideas, new answers. All this is inevitable and is to be welcomed as part of the process of growth.

Any spiritual commitment requires action. Such commitment must be demonstrated in one's personal life, of course. But, eventually, it requires social action as well. The time has come for the Bahá'í community to demonstrate, with concrete action in society, its commitment to universal and lasting international peace, to social justice, to spiritual values. It is an important moment in Bahá'í history. As the House of Justice put it:

> The time has come when those who preach the dogmas of materialism, whether of the east or the west, whether of capitalism or socialism, must give account of the moral stewardship they have presumed to exercise. Where is the "new world" promised by these ideologies? Where is the international peace to whose ideals they proclaim their devotion? Where are the breakthroughs into new realms of cultural achievement produced by the aggrandizement of this race, of that nation or of a particular class? Why is the vast majority of the world's peoples sinking ever deeper into hunger and wretchedness when wealth on a scale undreamed of by the Pharaohs, the Caesars, or even the imperialist powers of the nineteenth century is at the

disposal of the present arbiters of human affairs? (*The Promise of World Peace*, October 1985)

We must object, and bring to account, unjust acts or bellicose words or deeds carried out on the part of any nation or ideology, including our own.

AS BAHÁ'ÍS PURSUE this new task, they must not lose sight of their larger mission, the mission they regard as their unique obligation—to lay the foundations for the Most Great Peace, the spiritual transformation of humanity. For even after the nations put an end to war, profound troubles will continue to plague us. The world will be in need of active workers who can elaborate the moral dimensions of a hostile and unsteady peace. The challenge will be to create the ethical foundations for a united world; to build a new human identity that incorporates unity and peace at its center; to teach world citizenship, not as an ideal, but a reality; to lend popular and philosophical legitimacy to a new world order; to create world institutions; and to bring the full weight of sacred commitment to the new unity of the planet. This the Bahá'ís are preparing themselves to do.

THIS BOOK IS THE SECOND in a series of volumes to be published relating the Bahá'í Faith to current social issues. The first book, *Circle of Unity: Bahá'í Approaches to Current Social Issues*, was published in 1984. Other books are planned. These will include collections of essays on feminist issues, development issues, Marxism, international affairs, and so forth.

It should be emphasized that the essays in this volume represent only the views of their authors. They are not official statements of Bahá'í belief, nor do they represent the positions or attitudes of the institutions of the Bahá'í Faith. The reader will note that the various authors disagree with one another on a number of points. Their opinions carry no authority, of course. Anyone is free to disagree with any or all of them. Undoubtedly many will. The publisher welcomes letters and comments, even essays, in support or rebuttal to any article. Such responses will be forwarded to the appropriate authors.

Rather than being a final or comprehensive statement of Bahá'í beliefs, the purpose of these essays is to open the door to discussion within the Bahá'í community, and to pave the way for dialogue with other workers for peace. We maintain our confidence that through such a process of consultation and dialogue, the Bahá'í community will be strengthened in its new resolve and will offer powerful insights to the movement toward peace.

ANTHONY A. LEE
LOS ANGELES

CIRCLE OF PEACE
Reflections on the Bahá'í Teachings

Bahá'ís and American Peace Movements

by Richard Hollinger

IN RECENT MONTHS many Bahá'í communities in America have sponsored or participated in activities intended to promote world peace. Many more such activities are being contemplated by Bahá'ís in response to the United Nations declaration of 1986 as the International Year of Peace and the statement of the Universal House of Justice on peace. Such plans are a departure from Bahá'í practice in the immediate past, which avoided participation in almost any kind of political activity. Many Bahá'ís will be surprised to learn that, in the more distant past, the American believers actively participated in peace movements. This participation had the tacit, and sometimes explicit, approval of 'Abdu'l-Bahá and Shoghi Effendi. As we begin to plan such activities again, it will be instructive to look at the history of Bahá'í involvement in past peace movements.

Early in the twentieth century, prior to World War I, there was a thriving peace movement in the United States. Dozens of peace organizations with a variety of platforms competed, but the thrust of the movement was toward internationalism. Although few activists actually advocated world government, many supported the concept of a world court. Some wanted a series of treaties that would bind all nations—or at least a few of the more powerful ones—against an aggressor. Others advocated an international police force. The goals of the movement fell short of the Bahá'í teachings on peace but, in the context of the time, they represented a significant movement in the direction of Bahá'í ideals. They partially transcended the nationalism that dominated American thought in favor of a more international perspective.

Although the movement appears to have been fairly popular, it was not a grassroots movement. It was spawned and led by liberal businessmen and intellectuals in New England. It was primarily prominent and wealthy persons from this group who actively participated in it. A number of New England Bahá'ís were part of this elite social network, and contacts between Bahá'ís and peace activists were inevitable. As a result, a few individual Bahá'ís became involved in American peace organizations very early in the twentieth century.

However, collective participation by Bahá'ís in the movement does not seem to have begun until the time of 'Abdu'l-Bahá's visit to the West in 1911–1913, when His views on peace were articulated most clearly. Of course, Bahá'í concern with peace, having its origins in Bahá'u'lláh's writings, predates 'Abdu'l-Bahá's journey. But, after 'Abdu'l-Bahá left the Holy Land, He began to emphasize peace in His talks and writings more emphatically than He had done previously. The relationship between peace and other Bahá'í teachings (the equality of men and women, for example) was discussed. He repeatedly stressed the dangers of war, as well as the need to work for peace. For Bahá'ís—in the West, at least—this was a shift in emphasis. And Bahá'ís responded quickly.

In 1911, Charles Mason Remey represented the Bahá'ís at the Third Annual American Peace Conference, sponsored by the Church Peace Union in Baltimore. About the same time, Bahá'ís invited two important peace activists—Benjamin Trueblood, secretary of the American Peace Society (the largest American peace organization) and Fannie

Fern Andrews, secretary of the American School Peace League—to address a meeting in Washington, D.C. The occasion was the first conference of the Persian-American Educational Society, an organization founded by Bahá'ís primarily to create ties between America and Iran, but which also had other broad progressive goals. Among the resolutions that emerged from this conference was one endorsing a proposed arbitration treaty between the United States and England, and another urging China and Japan to open diplomatic relations with Iran. Benjamin Trueblood was elected vice-president of the society.[1]

In the same year, Mirza Ali Kuli Khan, a Bahá'í and the chargé d'affairs of the Persian consulate, related the Bahá'í teachings to the quest for peace in a talk given at the annual Mohonk Peace Conference.[2] This conference was first organized in the 1890s by Albert K. Smiley, a Quaker who rejected the pacifist teachings of his church and sought to establish world peace through more practical means. Every year Smiley invited prominent persons in education, business, and government to attend a conference at his hotel at Lake Mohonk in rural New York. This annual meeting had become a major forum for discussion and debate within the peace network and was a major force in establishing the movement among the New England elite. Largely as a result of this conference, a consensus began to emerge among peace activists that peace should be upheld by the threat of force against the aggressor—"enforced peace" they called it.

That a Bahá'í was invited to speak at this conference is itself significant. However, Ali Kuli Khan's appearance there may have been more important for the role it had in bringing 'Abdu'l-Bahá to Lake Mohonk—and to America. 'Abdu'l-Bahá learned of the conference not long after it took place, presumably from Ali Kuli Khan. Although he did not normally initiate correspondence with persons he did not know,[3] 'Abdu'l-Bahá made an exception for some American peace activists. In August 1911, he wrote to A. K. Smiley, and also to C. C. Phillips, the secretary of the Mohonk Conference, praising their work in the highest terms.[4] As a result, he received an invitation to speak at the conference the following year.

Contemporary newspaper articles cited attending the Mohonk conference as the purpose for 'Abdu'l-Bahá's visit to America.[5] 'Abdu'l-Bahá Himself identified invitations from peace conferences as the reason He decided to come. Undoubtedly there were other reasons but, upon His arrival in New York City He announced: "I have come to America to see the advocates of universal peace."[6]

Shortly after His arrival, 'Abdu'l-Bahá was greeted by the New York Peace Society—the most influential chapter of the American Peace Society—at a reception in His honor. Addressing this audience he proclaimed: *"Today there is no greater glory for man than that of service in the cause of the Most Great Peace. Peace is light, whereas war is darkness. Peace is life; war is death. Peace is guidance; war is error. Peace is the foundation of God; war is a satanic institution. Peace is the illumination of the world of humanity; war is the destroyer of human foundations."*[7]

The next day he arrived at the Mohonk Conference where He gave an address entitled "The Oneness of the Reality of Human Kind."[8] Most of the leading lights of the American peace movement had the opportunity to meet 'Abdu'l-Bahá at one of these two meetings. Others would meet Him later during His visit.

How much these leaders may have been influenced by 'Abdu'l-Bahá is something that Bahá'í historians will no doubt eventually wish to study in detail. It is clear from only a cursory examination of the events that the American Bahá'ís were dramatically affected by His talks, in which peace was one of the most common themes. 'Abdu'l-Bahá praised American efforts to negotiate an end to the Russo-Japanese war, a conflict which, though it was not well known in the West, had widespread effects in Asia. He urged further efforts of this kind. He charged Americans—Bahá'ís and others—to work for peace. He warned of a coming conflict in Europe, which He identified as the battle of Armageddon prophesied in the Bible. He also expressed His hope that America would not become involved in the war, but would emerge as a peacemaker.

In the wake of the Master's trip, Bahá'ís understood that they were obliged to work for peace, but they were not of one mind as to how to fulfill this duty. Some Bahá'ís felt that they should avoid the "worldly" peace movement, and argued that only spiritual activities, such as teaching the Faith, could bring peace. In this vein, one community suggested that all Bahá'ís should pray the Báb's prayer "the Remover of Difficulties" every morning and evening in order to bring about peace.[9] Other Bahá'ís, while not denying the value of prayer, advocated a more activist position. One group wanted to hold "mass meetings for peace wherever there is a Bahá'í center," offering a forum to "all peace parties on the broad Bahá'í Platform . . . "[10] Partially because of opposition within the Bahá'í community, this plan was not realized.

But Bahá'ís did not merely pray. Between the beginning of World War I, in 1914, and America's entry into the war, in April 1917, Bahá'ís promoted peace actively. Most agreed that they should support arbitration efforts—'Abdu'l-Bahá had been quite explicit in His support of these—so the Bahai Temple Unity, then the highest national Bahá'í body, telegraphed President Woodrow Wilson in support of his attempts to mediate the war in Europe.[11] Bahá'ís in Washington, D.C., published a small compilation of Bahá'í sacred writings on peace in one of the city's newspapers to garner support for the President's efforts. Later, this compilation was published as a booklet and a copy was sent to the White House.[12] Several Bahá'ís in northern California joined the American Neutral Conference Committee, a group which advocated even stronger efforts to mediate an end to the war.[13] One of these, Mrs. Phoebe Hearst, believing that women had a significant role to play in the peace movement, organized a women's peace conference which was held in San Francisco in 1915, about the same time as the (male dominated) Fifth Annual American Peace Conference. There were Bahá'í speakers at both conferences.[14]

The following year, Bahá'ís received an invitation from William Short—who met 'Abdu'l-Bahá in 1912—to send a delegation to the conference of the League to Enforce Peace. Formed by ex-President Taft in 1915, the League's platform was eventually accepted by President Wilson and adopted as the model for the League of Nations. Bahá'í delegates did attend the conference and assured the other attendees that they were "in full agreement with the League."[15]

With America's entry into the war, the peace movement became divided. Most prominent leaders and organizations —the New England peace establishment—supported the war effort. Convinced of the need for an "enforced peace," they argued that the United States was proceeding according to the principles that they had espoused all along. This was, after all, the "war to end war."

Some in the peace movement disagreed, however. Isolationists, pacifists, socialists, and others opposed American participation in the war for a wide variety of reasons. As war fever spread across the country, these people became increasingly isolated. Their spokesmen were mobbed, pelted with fruit, and threatened with lynchings at public meetings. Some were jailed without charges. The war was patriotic; peace had become a dirty word. Peace groups of all kinds were under suspicion, and their activities were examined closely by the government.

Bahá'ís were among those suspected of "seditious" activities. As Remey later recalled: "In those days everyone who belonged to a peace movement was under suspicion of being against the Government and this included the Bahá'ís in various places for hadn't the Master 'Abdu'l-Bahá talked on world peace while He was in America? And hadn't His followers staged peace rallies and urged world peace after He left this country?"[16] In New York City, Los Angeles, San Francisco, and elsewhere Bahá'ís were investigated by the Department of Justice. "Mother" Beecher, a well-known Bahá'í teacher, was arrested in Canada and expelled from the city where she was staying.[17] Edwin Fischer, a German-American Bahá'í, was arrested in Los Angeles on charges of espionage. He was accused of using the Bahá'í community as a spy network and a vehicle for pro-German propaganda. The charges were absurd, and they were eventually dismissed. But by then the Department of Justice had searched the office of the secretary of the Los Angeles Assembly, looking for evidence of a conspiracy. The Bahá'ís in Los Angeles felt compelled to stop holding meetings while the investigation was in progress, and Bahá'ís elsewhere were alarmed at the possibility of being viewed as political radicals.[18] Bahá'ís involved in the publication of a compilation on peace during the war feared that it might be confiscated as seditious material.[19] We now know that the Department of Justice continued investigating Bahá'ís into the 1920s and probably later.[20]

Under these circumstances, and being cut off from 'Abdu'l-Bahá by the war, it is not surprising that some Bahá'ís thought it wise to play down the Bahá'í teachings on peace, and to stress obedience to the government. Some even maintained that Bahá'ís must actively support the war effort. In the words of one Bahá'í who disagreed, they felt that "this was Bahá'u'lláh's war against Germany and it was the duty of every Bahá'í to support our Government in its war effort."[21] They argued that only by joining the war effort could the United States emerge as peacemaker—only then would America have a place at the conference table after the war. They pointed out that 'Abdu'l-Bahá had exhorted them to "yield not to the overwhelming tyranny and despotism. Serve the cause of democracy and freedom." And they asserted that the reason for American participation in the war was "so distinctly Bahá'í in its expression" that no Bahá'í could hesitate to serve in the military. They rejected the idea that Bahá'ís could be conscientious objectors.[22] Bahá'ís of this viewpoint dominated the executive board of the Bahai Temple Unity when, in August 1917, it sent a letter to the State Department pledging the support of the Bahá'ís for the war effort.[23]

Other Bahá'ís, however, felt that the community should remain neutral in the war—that the American war effort should not be endorsed. After August of 1917, Bahá'ís of this opinion began to mobilize support within the Bahá'í community against the letter to the State Department. At the 1918 national Convention, they succeeded in ousting the most pro-war members of the executive board, replacing them with persons sympathetic to their view. The board promptly rescinded the August 1917 statement, sending in its place a selection of Bahá'í writings on peace known as the *Compilation Concerning the Most Great Peace*.[24] The end of the war and renewed contact with 'Abdu'l-Bahá prevented the community from becoming permanently divided on this question, but the issues raised during this period would come up again.

Bahá'ís remained active in the peace movement after the war. They were especially active in their support for the concept of the League of Nations—even writing to President Wilson in France and meeting with his successor, Warren Harding, to express support for such an international institution.[25] In the late 1920s, the National Spiritual Assembly, the successor to the Bahai Temple Unity, embarked on a new venture which, though its primary purpose was teaching the Bahá'í Faith, was also seen as an attempt to influence public opinion and the peace movement in particular. This was the organization of a series of conferences (the first in 1925) on the theme of world unity, and in conjunction with this, the inauguration of the new magazine *World Unity*. These activities attracted the participation of prominent peace activists, such as David Starr Jordan and Lucia Ames Meade, and other leaders of thought who wished to promote an awareness of the need for the unification of the world.[26]

The conferences were expensive and not very successful as a teaching effort, however. In 1927, the National Assembly withdrew its official ties with the conferences, partly because of the financial burden they imposed on the community. Thereafter they were organized under the auspices of the World Unity Foundation.[27] Bahá'ís remained prominent in the leadership of the foundation though, and Bahá'í communities continued to support the conferences. They simply were not to be regarded as offical Bahá'í activities. In 1934, the National Assembly decided to make *World Unity* a fully Bahá'í journal, albeit one aimed largely at non-Bahá'í thinkers. In 1935, it became *World Order Magazine*.[28]

The 1930s were a time when American Bahá'ís were becoming more concerned with consolidating and expanding the Bahá'í community. This was, necessarily, at the expense of involvement in the larger society. This pattern the community would follow for several decades, and it resulted in a decline in peace activism.

We should note the historical context in which these changes took place. There were only about 2,000 American Bahá'ís in the 1930s, and some of the most active believers left the country to meet pioneering goals after the beginning of the first Seven Year Plan (1937). There were approximately 70 assemblies, and 260 localities open to the faith in this country.[29] The financial resources of the community were also quite limited, especially after the beginning of the Depression. This situation would not change dramatically until the 1960s.

Under such circumstances, Shoghi Effendi felt that the priorities of the American Bahá'í community should be the consolidation of the Administrative Order, expansion in the number of believers in this country, completion of the Bahá'í House of Worship in Illinois, and the spread of the Faith overseas. These objectives would consume all the human and financial resources the American Bahá'ís had for many years. What Bahá'ís might have done for the cause of peace was quite limited; it is highly unlikely that they could have contributed anything significant to the efforts to impede the rising militarism that eventually culminated in World War II.

Following the war, some Bahá'ís wanted to do something to promote peace, and they asked the National Spiritual Assembly to sponsor a "People's Peace Conference." The Guardian noted that "the idea and aims are excellent," but doubted that the Bahá'ís had the prestige, membership, or funds to successfully execute such a conference, so the National Assembly did not attempt this.[30] They did, however, write to the President and to the Department of State to voice support for the formation of the United Nations.[31]

Once the U.N. was formed, Bahá'ís supported it consistently and wholeheartedly. In 1947, the National Assembly began its work on behalf of the Bahá'ís of the world in the U.N. as a non-governmental agency. At a grassroots level, Bahá'ís promoted the United Nations through participation in United Nations Associations; observance of U.N. holidays; commemoration of special U.N. years (e.g., the International Year of Peace 1986); and the distribution of U.N. literature.

When the Vietnam antiwar movement developed in the 1960s, Bahá'ís did not become involved as a community. The National Assembly did advise Bahá'ís to seek noncombatant status in the Army, if they were drafted. (The experiences of one such conscientious objector are recounted elsewhere in this book.) But they did not want the name of the Faith associated with the antiwar movement. In 1969, they directed the Bahá'ís not to have any organized activities that would involve Bahá'ís in peace demonstrations, and instructed Bahá'ís not to attempt to teach the Faith at them.[32] The Assembly was probably concerned about how such actions might affect the Bahá'ís in Vietnam. The Faith had been outlawed in Vietnam, for a time, under the Diem regime, and this could have occurred again at any time.[33] There was undoubtedly also a concern about embroiling the community in one of the most divisive controversies in American history. In retrospect, these reasons may seem insufficient. But for those who lived through this turbulent era, it is easy to understand why there was a desire to avoid the controversy.

In the 1980s, another peace movement has emerged, this one more international in perspective. It has focused on the goal of slowing down or halting the arms race, especially the production of nuclear weapons. Like all peace movements, its objectives fall short of the goals of the Bahá'í teachings. But, the United Nations falls far short of the Bahá'í ideal of world government, and Bahá'ís support it as a move in the right direction. Bahá'ís would also be happy to slow down the arms race (short of unilateral disarmament). Therefore, they have begun to get involved in various peace organizations that have this aim. The statement of the Universal House of Justice on peace signaled the beginning of unprecedented contact between the Bahá'í community and the peace movement.

As we embark on renewed association with peace activists, we can learn from our past experiences as a community. There has never been anything wrong with participation in peace movements, so long as their goals are in accord with Bahá'í principles. 'Abdu'l-Bahá, our perfect Exemplar, was Himself a peace activist. It has been pragmatic considerations that have kept us away from such activities for certain periods of time. For example, it is clear that Bahá'ís were too few and uninfluential to make a difference in the 1930s; these are the same reasons Shoghi Effendi cited for not sponsoring a peace conference after World War II. There was nothing wrong, in principle, with sponsoring the conference as he noted.

Of course, the community was no larger in 1912, at the time of 'Abdu'l-Bahá's visit to the West, than it was in the 1930s. But the potential for peace was much greater then. Leading American political figures including Presidents Taft and Wilson, and Secretary of State Bryant, were members of a peace movement that gave rise to the League of Nations. The United States had emerged as a major power, but it was neutral in most affairs outside the Western hemisphere. America might have provided a unique force for peace, had it thrown its full weight behind the League of Nations. Peace appeared nearer in 1912 than it does in 1985.

It was not 'Abdu'l-Bahá's optimism that peace could be achieved that surprised people then; it was His prediction that it would be preceded by war in Europe. The very real possibility that political peace could be realized relatively quickly is probably what prompted 'Abdu'l-Bahá to exert His influence toward this end and to encourage Bahá'ís to do the same. By the 1930s this possibility was clearly gone.

Today the situation is different than it was in 'Abdu'l-Bahá's time, and different from the 1930s. The United States is no longer a neutral power. Since World War II, America has become a major actor on the world scene, exerting its influence in pursuit of its own interests. The Soviet Union has emerged as America's chief rival. These two Superpowers have engaged in the largest arms buildup in human history; they supply massive amounts of weapons to their allies, thus encouraging armed conflict around the world. The military-industrial complex has become a major force in American society. In the Soviet Union the military has become perhaps the most powerful political force in the country; military expenditures account for more of the Soviet Gross National Product than U.S. expenditures do for the American GNP. Only the threat of mutually assured destruction has kept these two massive military establishments from a head-on collision.

The peace movement reflects this new reality. Its goals are very limited—reducing military spending; freezing the development of nuclear weapons; possibly eventually reducing the arms buildup. This is probably the most that it can realistically expect to accomplish in the near future; the social forces supporting the arms race are just too strong to hope for much more. The objectives of the peace movement are definitely positive, but from a Bahá'í point of view they are far too limited. We would like to see the development of world institutions that will actually result in the establishment of a permanent peace.

The American Bahá'í community is also in a different situation than it was at the time of 'Abdu'l-Bahá or during the Guardian's time. Most of the goals that Shoghi Effendi envisioned for the American community have now been met: the Faith has spread around the world; the House of Worship has been completed; the Administrative Order has been erected; the community has expanded dramatically. The financial resources of the Bahá'í community have also grown. Today there are more than 95,000 Bahá'ís on the rolls in this country—almost fifty times the number in the 1930s!

United, and relatively well organized, Bahá'ís represent a potentially powerful force within the American peace movement. We are now in a position not just to support such efforts, but to influence their future direction. The peace movement consists largely of local grassroots organizations, which have little contact with one another. Peace activists readily acknowledge that the movement lacks vision, direction, and leadership, especially at a national level. In my experience, peace activists readily recognize the wisdom of the Bahá'í teachings on peace, if they are presented to them intelligently. Some local peace organizations have been influenced by the Bahá'í teachings to the extent that they have expanded their goals to include such things as the elimination of prejudice and the equality of men and women. If every active Bahá'í in this country joined a peace organization, we could have a tremendous influence on the movement. We might even be able to put world federalism on the long-term agenda of the movement.

This would be a significant accomplishment. We must

realize that this peace movement, like the ones before it, will probably not last for more than a few years. It is very unlikely that it will bring peace to the world. But Bahá'ís, as an article of faith, must be committed to a long-term struggle for peace—we will be involved in this struggle until it is successful. If we can plant the idea in the popular culture, by way of the peace movement, that world government is a prerequisite of world peace, this will be an important step toward lasting peace. Ideas have a way of staying around longer than movements do, and of taking on a life of their own. If we are able to do this, the wisdom of world government may be increasingly recognized. And then, when peace movements arise in the future, they will have to address this issue.

Bahá'ís understand that the struggle to bring about world peace may be a long one. Efforts of the past—both Bahá'í activities and peace movements—have not been able to bring about peace. And we cannot be sure just when peace will be achieved. As the Guardian observed: " . . . All we know is that the Lesser and the Most Great Peace *will* come—their exact dates we do not know."[34] Again he noted: "World government will come, but we do not know the date."[35] Recognizing that questions of *how* and *when* are always conditioned on human actions, we must do our part to see that it comes about as quickly and as painlessly as possible.

NOTES

1. Charles Mason Remey, "The Bahá'í Movement: A Teaching of Peace," *Star of the West*, vol. II, no. 5, pp. 9–13. "Persian-American Educational Society," *Star of the West*, vol. II, nos. 7–8, pp. 3–7.

2. *Report of the Seventeenth Annual Lake Mohonk Conference on International Arbitration* (Lake Mohonk Conference: 1911) pp. 79–85.

3. This was the conclusion of Dr. Vahid Rafati based on a review of 1,400 tablets of 'Abdu'l-Bahá in the National Bahá'í Archives. See Notes of the Los Angeles Bahá'í Study Class, vol. II, no. 16 (November 27, 1977).

4. "Tablets from Abdul Baha" *Star of the West*, vol. II, no. 15 (December 1911) pp. 3–5.

5. "Leader of Bahais to Visit Here," *Pittsburgh Press* March 24, 1912. "Persian Quits Prison; Here to Fight for Peace," *New York Evening Telegram*, April 11, 1912. "Abdul Baha Here," *New York Times*, April 12, 1912. "Abdul Baha Prays in Ascencion Church," *New York Times*, April 15, 1912.

6. "Disciples Here Hail Abdul Baha," *New York Sun*, April 12, 1912. The Diary of Mahmúd-i Zarqání, translation in the National Bahá'í Archives, pp. 28, 34. The quote is taken from page 34 of the translation.

7. *The Promulgation of Universal Peace* (Wilmette: Bahá'í Publishing Trust, 1982) p. 123. On this meeting, see also *Star of the West* vol. III, no. 8, pp. 10–15.

8. Guest book of the Lake Mohonk Mountain House, entry for May 14, 1912. 'Abdu'l-Bahá's address to this conference may be found in *Report of the Eighteenth Annual Lake Mohonk Conference on International Arbitration* (Lake Mohonk Conference: 1912) pp. 42–44.

9. San Francisco Bahá'í Assembly to the Bahá'í Assemblies of America, September 9, 1914. San Francisco Bahá'í Archives.

10. Peace Committee of the Bahai Temple Unity to the San Francisco Bahá'í Assembly, September 6, 1916. San Francisco Bahá'í Archives.

11. "Bahai Temple Unity Convention," *Star of the West*, vol. v, no. 10 (September 8, 1914) p. 150.

12. Ahmad Sohrab, comp., *The Most Great Peace* (Boston: Tudor Press, 1916). The copy of this in the Library of Congress has an inscription indicating that it was transferred from the White House library.

13. Letterhead of the American Neutral Conference Committee, A. K. Smiley Papers, Smiley Library. The Bahá'ís listed on the letterhead are Phoebe Hearst, Anthony Caminetti, and Phillip K. Brown.

14. May Wright Sewall, *Women, World War and Permanent*

Peace. (San Francisco: John J. Newbegin, 1915). The original plans for the women's peace conference are in the Phoebe Hearst Papers at the Bancroft Library. On the other conference, see *Advocate of Peace* (October 1915) p. 224; November 1915, pp. 243-245; and *Proceedings of the Fifth American Peace Congress held in San Francisco, California, October 10-13, 1915* (New York: Church Peace Union, 1915).

15. Letter from Charles Mason Remey dated June 1, 1916 in *Bahá'í Reminiscences, diary, letters and other documents by Charles Mason Remey*, volume 39, New York Public Library.

16. Charles Mason Remey. *Reminiscences of the Summer School Green-Acre Eliot, Maine* (Haifa?:1955) p. 81.

17. Charles Mason Remey. *A Report to Abdul Baha of the Bahai Activities in the States of North Carolina, South Carolina, Georgia, and Florida, U.S.A.* (Washington, D.C.: 1919) p. 1.

18. Criminal Case File 1540, United States National Archives, Laguna Niguel Regional Branch. "Big Catch by Government?" *Los Angeles Times*, September 5, 1918, p. 1. Frank Beckett to Helen Goodall (n.d.), Ella Cooper papers, San Francisco Bahá'í Archives. Willard Hatch, "Early Days in Los Angeles Bahá'í Affairs," National Bahá'í Archives.

19. Remey, *Reminiscences of the Summer School*, pp. 82-83.

20. I am indebted to Mr. David Piff for this information, which is based on his research in the Department of Justice records at the United States National Archives.

21. Remey, *Reminiscences of the Summer School*, p. 78.

22. San Francisco Bahá'í Assembly to the Assemblies in America, August 7, 1917, Chicago House of Spirituality papers, National Bahá'í Archives. Proposal for statement on the Bahá'í attitude towards the government, San Francisco Bahá'í Archives.

23. "A Communication to the Government at Washington," *Star of the West*, vol. VIII, no. 12, pp. 153-156.

24. Remey, *Reminiscences of the Summer School*, p. 80. Charles Mason Remey to Claudia Coles, Mary Rabb, and Ella Cooper, October 24, 1918, in *Bahá'í Reminiscences, diary, letters, and other documents*, vol. 41. The full title of the compilation is *9 Compilation of the Holy Utterances of Baha'o'llah and Abdul Baha Concerning the Most Great Peace, War and Duty of the Bahais toward their Government*.

25. George Orr Latimer, *The Lesser and the Most Great Peace* (Wilmette: Bahá'í Publishing Committee, 1944) p. 16. Letter from Charles Mason Remey dated 1921, Ella Cooper Papers, San Francisco Bahá'í Archives.

26. This information was gleaned from various issues of *World Unity*.

27. *Bahá'í News* (November 27, 1927) p. 5. Gayle Morrison, *To Move the World* (Wilmette: Bahá'í Publishing Trust, 1982) p. 161.

28. *Bahá'í News* (January 1935) p. 1.

29. In the mid-1930s the N.S.A. sent Historical Record Cards out to Bahá'í communities to be filled out by each Bahá'í. About 1,800 were filled out and are in the National Bahá'í Archives. Not every Bahá'í who got one filled it out, of course, and isolated believers are likely to have been overlooked.

The U.S. Religious Census of 1936 indicates that there were 2,584 Bahá'ís. But the method of gathering figures for the census was such that this is likely to have been an exaggeration. Figures for Assemblies and localities come from *Bahá'í News* May 1936, p. 12.

30. *Bahá'í News* (April–May 1945) p. 2.

31. Ibid., p. 13.

32. "In Time of Peace Demonstrations," *National Bahá'í Review* (December 1969) p. 1.

33. "American Bahá'ís Key to Peace in Vietnam," *The American Bahá'í* (November 1970) p. 3.

34. Research Department of the Universal House of Justice comp. *Establishing World Peace* (Parnell, New Zealand: National Spiritual Assembly of the Bahá'ís of New Zealand, 1985) p. 48.

35. Ibid., p. 46.

World Peace: The Dream in Daylight

by Robert T. Phillips

> *Whatever you can do, or dream you can, begin it.*
> *Boldness has genius, power and magic in it.*
> Goethe

IT IS TIME FOR A CHANGE. The facts are known. Wars, ecological disasters, economic collapse, famine, nuclear winter, urban decay, adversarial human relationships, and the loss of irreplaceable resources are the bitter fare of our daily news. We seem to have evolved a global society determined to choose death over life in ever increasing doses. Death packaged as defense, good business, ideology, modern technology, and national security. It is clear that such factors as an expanding global population, rapid advances in military technology, and a pervasive spirit of materialistic nationalism have combined to create an age characterized by the largest scale of human misery and mismanagement known to history. Our reach has exceeded our grasp.

We live on an earth that is obviously, visually one, but is not yet whole. In the search for peace, for a change from omnipresent war and violence, who speaks for humanity? Who speaks for the human spirit across the ages? Who acts as trustee for the unborn children of our species, for the suddenly vulnerable creatures of the earth, for the earth itself?

There are many voices for change, many groups organized for reform. Most prepare a plan or a constitution and lobby for its acceptance. Often these are legalistic or moral approaches that seem either judgmental or out of touch with the realities of our time. They alienate or fail to move all but their own supporters. Are Bahá'ís different?

The Bahá'í Faith is not simply a peace plan or a blueprint for future society, though it contains those things. It does not simply chronicle the world's ills in the hope that the recitation of enough terror, misery, or hardship will somehow impel change and inspire peace. Peace, in the Bahá'í view, is not a product, a thing that can be independently learned, or merely an alternative to war. It is rather the result of a process, the goal of the evolution of our species, the culmination of the purpose of our existence. It is the newborn child of a renewed faith, the rebirth of religion. Bahá'u'lláh wrote: *"That which the Lord hath ordained as the sovereign remedy and mightiest instrument for the healing of all the world is the union of all its peoples in one universal Cause, one common Faith."*[1]

Such a total change, the creation of a world religion, is without precedent. It is change on a level unheard of and, for many, still unthinkable. *Bahá'í* is the name given to some of the people who have started to think and act on this change. Yet, as we look at those few Bahá'ís and their efforts, we have to ask is it enough—soon enough, big enough, powerful enough? Beyond announcing the Bahá'í Faith and its principles and attracting the belief in them by several million people, what next? What new steps lie on the path, within the process, to peace? As Lazlo put the question: "How do potential recruits in a world-order movement circumvent the many obstacles that now block the road to global reform? How does such a movement mobilize enough energy to reorganize the world system without first gaining control over the apparatus of the state in most of the important countries of the world?"[2]

First of all, it is useful to abandon those illusions instilled into us by our various national cultures about the real sources of a future at peace. National movements in Africa, Latin America, Asia, Europe, and America have bankrupted their economies with military expenditures that have reached 663 billion dollars worldwide (1983) and represent a theft of food, health, education, shelter and jobs from their own people. Ideologies such as communism, capitalism, socialism and Islamic fundamentalism have all failed to deliver on their promises of egalitarian, free and prosperous societies. Indeed it is often these governments themselves that are the foremost obstacles to the realization of the basic freedoms and needs of their people. Tragically, it is history that these "saviors" of their people have slaughtered millions of their own in external wars or internal persecution in the last forty years. Kampuchea, Honduras, Iran, Uganda, Chile, Afganistan, Vietnam, Argentina, the United States, Lebanon, the USSR, Brazil, China, Ethiopia, Ireland, and South Africa are only some of a long litany of those countries which, in pursuit of national aims, have deprived their own citizens and/or their so-called enemies of property, food, liberty, education, and life itself. In the ultimate expression of the bankruptcy of nationalism, the entire planet is held hostage to the great power rivalry between the United States and the Soviet Union and their allies. Held hostage by the intensely personal threat of over fifty thousand nuclear weapons poised on armadas of ships, satellites, missiles, and planes ready to annihilate each other, and possibly the planet, to preserve their respective sovereignties and privileged way of life. It is time for a change.

Yet, are there not answers left untried, time still for negotiation? As the Guardian of the Bahá'í Faith observed:

Every system, short of the unification of the human race, has been tried, repeatedly tried, and been found wanting. Wars again and again have been fought, and conferences without number have met and deliberated. Treaties, pacts and covenants have been painstakingly negotiated, concluded and revised. Systems of government have been patiently tested, have been continually recast and superseded. Economic plans of reconstruction have been carefully devised, and meticulously executed. And yet crisis has succeeded crisis, and the rapidity with which a perilously unstable world is declining has been correspondingly accelerated. A yawning gulf threatens to involve in one common disaster both the satisfied and dissatisfied nations, democracies and dictatorships, capitalists and wage-earners, Europeans and Asiatics, Jew and Gentile, white and colored.[3]

Why this suffering, these calamities that threaten to engulf us? Again the Guardian explains:

In the spiritual development of man a stage of purgation is indispensable, for it is while passing through it that the over-rated material needs are made to appear in their proper light. Unless society learns to attribute more importance to spiritual matters, it would never be fit to enter the golden era foretold by Bahá'u'lláh. The present calamities are parts of this process of purgation, through them alone will man learn his lesson. They are to teach the nations, that they have to view things internationally, they are to make the individual attribute more importance to his moral, than his material welfare.

In such a process of purgation, when all humanity is in the throes of dire suffering, the Bahá'ís should not hope to remain unaffected. Should we consider the beam that is in our own eye, we would immediately find that these sufferings are also meant for ourselves, who claimed to have attained. Such world crisis is necessary to awaken us to the importance of our duty and the carrying on of our task. Suffering will increase our energy in setting before humanity the road to salvation, it will move us from our repose for we are far from doing our best in teaching the Cause and conveying the Message with which we have been entrusted.[4]

World Peace: The Vision. The difficulty with peace, with doing something concrete to achieve it, has been that the goal has often seemed too diffuse, too remote to be affected by individual activity. Diffuse in that it is not one thing, a single activity, or a concrete possession that we can obtain and say: Now, we have peace. Remote in that there seems always to have been war, and since war is conducted by governments and generals, is not peace also exclusively within their power? Remote also in the apparent lack of real progress toward peace.

It is imperative to recognize that peace does not come from declaring war on the warriors or from banning their nuclear bombs, chemical or germ weapons, planes, ships, or tanks. The human mind is endlessly inventive and has irrevocably unlocked the secrets of a technology that is global in scope. No peace plan that fails to illumine and transform the mind and spirit behind that technology will ever succeed in transforming its destructive products and their uses. The power to recreate minds and spirits, therefore, lies at the heart of the struggle for peace. Bahá'ís and others concerned with the creation of world peace can learn and act on the fact that that power, that ability to mount and sustain meaningful action, does not rest with those who claim it today. We can clearly see in the record of today's governments their complete failure to meet the world's urgent need for peace. Power lies in the hands of those who act in unity, using the spiritual principles and institutions revealed by Bahá'u'lláh.

The Bahá'í Writings promote and inspire a vision, a new

consciousness. Bahá'u'lláh says, *"The earth is but one country and mankind its citizens . . . Let not a man glory in this, that he loves his country; let him rather glory in this, that he loves his kind."*[5] Matched with the science-born image of our planet alive and vibrant in space is Bahá'u'lláh's spiritual vision, shimmering on the edge of our understanding and giving us a new sense of who we are and why we are here. That vision speaks through the Bahá'í Writings in practical details of a world government—a world legislature and tribunal; a world language, script and currency; the equality of men and women; the abolition of racism; disarmament and collective security. All of these are preconditions to the establishment of a lasting peace. Yet, that spiritual vision is stillborn unless we give it the nurturance of not only belief, but also of action.

World Peace: Teaching It. Seen thus, our responsibility toward the starvation, poverty, prejudice, violence, and exploitation in the world is to change the nationalistic, materialistic, racist, sexist, and exploitative attitudes and values which are the source of such suffering. Bahá'ís call that *teaching*, sharing in a spirit of love " . . . on a global scale and to every stratum of human society . . . the healing message that the Promised One has come and that the unity and well-being of the human race is the purpose of His Revelation."[6]

Such teaching may begin on the level of the purpose of God for man, yet it will not endure if it remains there. People, Bahá'ís and others, live out their existence in a sequence of daily decisions about work, relationships, food, children, housing, entertainment, etc. Change, meaningful change, occurs through altering the substance of those daily decisions whose aggregate today is more productive of the world's problems than its solutions. Peace will result when Bahá'ís, and those who seek peace, change the substance of their decisions. It is time for a change.

Yet some would say, and with reason, that many groups have outstripped Bahá'í communities in their adoption of non-violent lifestyles, of solar energy, of healthy practices and antinuclear programs. What is critically different about the Bahá'í approach is that it begins with and originates from universal spiritual principles, rather than pragmatic responses to individual issues. Things will work in a global age when they are in harmony with global principles and global needs—when we "think globally, act locally." This is not to negate the importance of individual activities confined to a particular concern. Rather it is to state the truth that daily action, to be of enduring effect, must be inspired and guided by universal principles, must reflect a larger reality. It is also true that those guided by the principles revealed by Bahá'u'lláh have an awesome responsibility to manifest not only the power of a growing world community of believers, but also the daily differences those principles make to the quality of personal decisions.

World Peace: The Opportunity. Personal contact with war, failed relationships, economic hardship, racial unrest, changing sex roles and the myriad other changes and trials of our times tends to purge individuals of their attachments to old values and beliefs. Thus released, millions of people are, many for the first time, searching for solutions: searching for a way to integrate their individuality, their capacities, their needs with an age thoroughly out of balance. The Universal House of Justice, in a 1969 letter, described it thus:

> In the worsening world situation, fraught with pain of war, violence and the sudden uprooting of long-established institutions, can be seen the fulfillment of the prophecies of Bahá'u'lláh and the oft-repeated warnings of the Master and the beloved Guardian about the inevitable fate of a lamentably defective social system, an unenlightened leadership and a rebellious and unbelieving humanity.

Governments and peoples of both the developed and developing nations, and other human institutions, secular and religious, finding themselves helpless to reverse the trend of the catastrophic events of the day, stand bewildered and overpowered by the magnitude and complexity of the problems facing them. . . . Nevertheless a greater and greater number of thoughtful and fair-minded men and women are recognizing in the clamour of contention, grief and destruction, now reaching such horrendous proportions, the evidences of Divine chastisement, and turning their faces towards God are becoming increasingly receptive to His Word. Doubtless the present circumstances, though tragic and awful in their immediate consequences, are serving to sharpen the focus on the indispensability of the Teachings of Bahá'u'lláh to the needs of the present age, and will provide many opportunities to reach countless waiting souls, hungry and thirsty for Divine guidance."[7]

This opportunity can be translated from the general to the specific by the efforts of Bahá'ís and their colleagues and by the responses of the Bahá'í Administrative Order. Let us first examine, as examples, a few of the areas of potentially fruitful activity, and then relate those possibilities to the role of individuals and Bahá'í Administration in the process of creating world peace.

Economics: Working Toward Peace. As materialistic values are dominant in both capitalistic and socialist/communist systems, it is here that the scale of disillusionment and physical suffering is at its height. And here that the opportunity for effective Bahá'í activity is great.

Many thoughtful people have realized that in our drive to build materially affluent, consumer-oriented societies, we have entered into a destructive relationship with nature and the natural resources that are used to create a high material standard of living. Here it is an attitude that is at fault—the Western man's attitude, increasingly accepted by national leaders throughout the world, that we are not part of nature but an external force whose ascendency is based on the power to conquer nature and to exploit it. We have lost touch with the reality that our natural resources are finite: fossil fuels, minerals, grasslands, forests, oceans, and air are not human creations, but are rather the divine "capital" with which we are entrusted. Bahá'ís and others who seek peace will necessarily erect economic enterprises and undertake productive activities based on quite different principles.

As E. F. Schumaker suggests:

> We must thoroughly understand the problem and begin to see the possibility of evolving a new life style, with new methods of production and new patterns of consumption: a life-style designed for permanence. To give only three preliminary examples: in agriculture and horticulture, we can interest ourselves in the perfection of production methods which are biologically sound, build up soil fertility, and produce health, beauty and permanence. Productivity will then look after itself. In industry, we can interest ourselves in the evolution of small-scale technology, relatively non-violent technology, "technology with a human face," so that people have a chance to enjoy themselves while they are working, instead of working solely for their pay packet and hoping, usually forlornly, for enjoyment solely during their leisure time. In industry, again—and, surely, industry is the pace-setter of modern life—we can interest ourselves in new forms of partnership between management and men, even forms of common ownership."[8]

The point here is that peace is not a product of economic prosperity, but rather of harmony, living and working in harmony with nature and each other.

One of the ways to reduce tensions that lead to war is to reduce the material demands and artificially created "needs" for goods and services that are the source of these tensions. Bahá'ís can become the source of a new, nondestructive productivity. As 'Abdu'l-Bahá states:

> *O ye friends, exert ye an effort! Every expenditure is in need of an income. This day, in the world of humanity, men are all the time expending, for war is nothing but the consumption of men and of wealth. At least engage ye in a deed of profit to the world of humanity that ye may partially compensate for that loss.*[9]

This would suggest to me that Bahá'ís, their families, friends and associates might:

☐ become involved, when possible, in agricultural projects that utilize organic farming methods. Such projects can range from individual backyard or apartment gardens to full scale commercial enterprises. It would seem especially appropriate for Bahá'ís to seek distinction here. As Bahá'u'lláh in writing of the principles to guide human affairs stated: *"Special regard must be paid to agriculture. Although it hath been mentioned in the fifth place* [preceded by statements on the Lesser Peace, one common language, promotion of unity, and payment for child education], *unquestionably it precedeth the others."*[10] Bahá'í schools and centers could play a leadership role for the Bahá'í and non-Bahá'í community alike by integrating agricultural training into their curriculum and sponsoring demonstration projects aiming at both the provision of healthy produce for the school or center and the generation of income through commercial sale.

☐ seek to utilize renewable resources for their energy needs and minimize their reliance on fossil fuels through fuel efficient cars and a reduction in the number of household appliances. Solar energy and wood burning stoves are just a few of the alternative energy sources available for exploration and experimentation.

☐ become involved in work that is of service and helps to make a whole, unified life, not just a salary. Marilyn Ferguson states in *The Aquarian Conspiracy*: "Our hunger turns out to be for something different, not something more. Buying, selling, owning, saving, sharing, keeping, investing, giving—these are outward expressions of inward needs. When those needs change, as in personal transformation, economic patterns change."[11] Just what those changes might be for our personal economic life is as individual as each of us, and must often take time and patience to achieve. 'Abdu'l-Bahá identifies the characteristics of the work we should seek: *"Again, is there any deed in the world that would be nobler than service to the common good? Is there any greater blessing conceivable for a man, than that he should become the cause of the education, the development, the prosperity and honor of his fellow-creatures?"*[12] Education, health promotion, agriculture, nonmilitary science, and the arts are just a few of the fields which can enable Bahá'ís to work in unity, in service, and to model the peace generating principles of their Faith.

One other innovation which would be a dramatic change from current practice and would help to alleviate part of the unjust and unequitable distribution of wealth in contemporary society would be a plan to enable both rich and poor to have equal access to Bahá'í meetings, pilgrimages, conferences, and schools. Generally, minority and Third World peoples are effectively eliminated from attendance at these events due to the costs, which often presume a middle-class income. If we are to change our society through the application of spiritual principles to current issues, recognition that the roots of middle-class abundance rest partially in the exploitation and impoverishment of minority and Third World peoples is crucial. It is time for a change.

A change here, one already developed by some groups, could deal with travel costs, often the major and most inequitable expense for a national conference or summer school. These costs could be shared equally among all attendees by asking each person to determine how much they can afford above or below the average travel cost, depending on evaluation of their personal resources. The event itself can be structured so that options, from camping to hotels, are available. Thus, no one is economically excluded. (My purpose here is not to advocate a particular system or plan to eliminate economic inequity, but to suggest that Bahá'ís have a particular duty to be conscious of and take responsibility for the fact that the seeds of war are often nourished by the way we regard and use our economic resources. This same analysis can be used to examine current practices that might have the unconscious effect of continuing racism and racial separation, sexism and the denial of the rightful place of women in some Bahá'í functions.)

Health: The Body At Peace. While we may feel powerless to affect summit negotiations between superpowers, we do have control over our own bodies. In each of our physical beings we find a mirror of, a connection to, our spiritual essence. 'Abdu'l-Bahá states that: *"Between material things and spiritual things there is a connection. The more healthful his body the greater will be the power of the spirit of man; the power of the intellect, the power of the memory, the power of reflection will then be greater."*[13] People who do violence to their own selves through smoking, poor diet, stress, lack of exercise, and exposure to toxic environments may be less sensitive to and therefore more capable of violence toward others and to the environment. One commentator put it thus:

> The complex interplay of animate and inanimate systems on the surface of the earth—soil, air, water, plants and animals—has come only recently to be appreciated as a delicate but fundamental factor in the welfare of the

planet. We have just begun to realize that our unthinking interaction with these systems—air, soil and water—multiplied by families and groups and cities and crowds can burden them and shift them from a state of equilibrium, the thrust of which can recoil, damaging us, our food supply and our health in turn.[14]

All human beings can become, therefore, more harmonious, more unified, more peaceful, and more persuasive as models of peace if they begin to change their health habits by:

☐ attuning their diet toward vegetarianism and away from reliance on sugars, processed foods, and red meats. Our digestive tract is our inside skin, our source of intimate and constant interaction with our world. It is literally the way we internalize our existence. An imbalance in our being can manifest itself in overeating, improper eating, or other disorders that result in disease. Bahá'ís, in their personal diets and at their communal meetings such as Feasts, conferences, schools, etc., can make meaningful change toward peace simply by serving healthy foods and not the sugary, processed and high cholesterol fare that too often characterize our daily diets and social functions. Much is known and available concerning good nutrition and can be put to immediate use.
☐ avoiding smoking and developing clear policies that discourage smoking, helping smokers quit and protecting nonsmokers at all Bahá'í functions.
☐ promoting regular aerobic exercise both in our personal life and as an integral part of all appropriate Bahá'í functions.
☐ ensuring that health promotion training is an important part of the education given to children and youth at all Bahá'í schools. Healthy habits are much easier to set properly at an early stage, than to correct in adulthood.
☐ actively considering health promotion as a fruitful area

for social development projects, realizing both the intrinsic impact of the promotion of physical health on spiritual growth and the teaching potential of contacts made in such a positive context.

☐ ensuring that birth and death are acknowledged and respected as healthy and natural experiences characterized by a spirit of love and peace. Too often birth is in a cold hospital with drugged babies pulled from drugged mothers into the shock of bright lights, strangers, and loud noises—with no possibility of bonding between child and family. Too many American births are caesarean operations, often proved unnecessary and performed frequently for the convenience and profit of physician and hospital. Bahá'ís and their families can take powerful and practical steps toward beginning life in peace by ensuring that birth occurs in a way that creates family unity and bonding, by use of birth centers, midwives, home births, and other procedures that acknowledge the spiritual essence of the event and the rights of both baby and parents. Death, for many, takes place in the impersonal isolation of nursing homes or geriatric hospital wards—warehouses for castoff people. Dying and death are natural passage, a fulfillment, a messenger of joy, rather than a medical failure to be fought with intrusive technology. Bahá'ís can utilize their Assembly and family resources when a loved one is dying and become involved in hospice programs. How we handle birth and death will greatly influence the quality and the peace potential of the time between the two.

All these suggestions, and the many others that are prompted by the principles involved, are useful to the extent that the Bahá'ís involved are themselves actively involved in and committed to the health promoting changes that are the focus of the program.

Bahá'í Administration: Organizing For Peace. To this point we have focused on the changes in consciousness that are the foundation of world peace and the changes in the substance of personal decisions and behavior that erect the structure of peace on that foundation. What is missing is an analysis of the role of Bahá'í Administration in the creation of world peace. The Guardian of the Bahá'í Faith wrote of the importance of the Bahá'í Administrative Order and the need for Bahá'ís to "understand its purpose and all it can achieve once they get it to function properly. . . . It is the ideal instrument to make spiritual laws function properly in the material affairs of this world."[15]

At the same time, the Bahá'í Writings state that this embryonic global government must be characterized by a unifying spirit and an openness to change. Unlike other political systems whose goals quickly become their own preservation and privilege, the Guardian insisted that "the whole machinery of [Bahá'í] assemblies, of committees and conventions is to be regarded as a means, and not an end in itself; that they will rise or fall according to their capacity to further the interests, to coordinate the activities, to apply the principles, to embody the ideals and execute the purpose of the Bahá'í Faith."[16] That primary purpose, essential to the establishment of peace, is to promote the teaching of the spiritual principles of the Bahá'í Faith—a process necessary for changing the consciousness and attitudes of the peoples of the world.

There is a simplicity about the process of sharing the Bahá'í message with your fellow human. He or she either accepts it or does not. If Bahá'í administrative bodies organize activities properly and individual Bahá'ís respond in love and unity, then large numbers of people will be attracted, the Bahá'í community will grow, and the process of peace will be advanced. The Universal House of Justice clearly identifies this growth as the precursor to the creation of a new world order and to world peace: "When the masses of mankind are awakened and enter the Faith of God, a new process is set in motion and the growth of a new civilization begins."[17] In the last few years in America, and in much of the so-called developed world, such growth on a large scale has not happened. As the Universal House of Justice wrote in its 1984 message to the Bahá'ís of the United States, "... we cannot help noticing the sad lag in the rate of your enrollments, a lag which is conspicuously at variance with the high energy of your endeavors and the teaching opportunities abounding in your richly blessed land.... The progress of the Cause in your country undoubtedly depends on such expansion."

As the present structure of committees and conferences, locally and nationally—both in the United States and some other countries, does not seem to be as productive as possible, significant changes would seem appropriate and might include such options as follows:

☐ if the local or national system of projects, committees and meetings is not producing growth and achieving the goals, give active consideration to abolishing them. Find those projects, individuals, centers, and communities that are productive and commit spiritual and physical resources to expand and export that success. Dramatic change itself can often stimulate a dormant community.

☐ utilize the global interest in peace stimulated by the United Nation's 1985–1986 International Year of Peace. Bahá'ís can actively collaborate with other groups working for peace to sponsor events, especially those which can present the October 1985 call of the Universal House of Justice for a convocation of the world's leaders to lay the foundation of world peace. Working together with other groups broadens the base of contacts and stimulates Bahá'ís by exposing them to teaching opportunities with those who are already committed to the concept of peace.

☐ in this regard, it is useful to remember that organizations concerned with such issues as national defense, the environment, racial justice, women's rights, apartheid in South Africa, economic development, and so forth are peace groups. The successful resolution of these issues, among others, is the foundation upon which peace can be built. However liberal or conservative their respective expression of commitment to these issues, Bahá'ís should not exclude such groups from consideration as potential collaborators unless extreme partisanship or unethical behavior characterize their activities.

Indeed, unity in diversity as a spiritual principle presumes that Bahá'ís and others who are similarly committed to world unity must make every effort to bring together the full spectrum of opinion on the various issues and concerns that contribute to world peace. Thus, the Chamber of Commerce, the Rotary Club, the V.F.W., and the Teamsters Union are as likely collaborators as are the Unitarians, Beyond War, the NAACP, or university student clubs.

☐ activities which accomplish, improve or create some tangible benefit or service are much more exciting than the normal "call-a-meeting—get-a-speaker—serve-refreshments" model. The Universal House of Justice, in its October 20, 1983 message to the Bahá'ís of the world spoke of the beginning of a whole new dimension in the relationship between the Bahá'í community and the larger society. This means, in its words, " . . . greater involvement in the development of the social and economic life of peoples." While the experience of the many existing Bahá'í development projects are primary sources of information for anyone entering this field, it is useful in the context of peace activities to note that these activities commit Bahá'ís to a very different relationship to the communities in which they live. Heretofore, Bahá'ís have focused primarily on personal belief and individual attributes. Now we are challenged to put these beliefs to work transforming the social and economic conditions around us. Only then will we have a foundation which will sustain a New World Order.

Such development begins with a candid appraisal of our own Bahá'í communities to ensure that conditions of social or economic deprivation do not exist. If they do, move to alleviate them. Operating from the base of a unified and developed Bahá'í community, we can then evaluate the needs of our local area, match those with the talents, resources and interests of the Bahá'ís and their collaborators and begin work on the projects which emerge from this analysis.

World Peace: The Dream In Daylight. Finally, no treatment of the establishment of peace, after October 1985, is able to ignore the historic letter of the Universal House of Justice to the peoples of the world. In a global assertion of its station as Trustee of Bahá'u'lláh's Revelation, it publicly states that: "The Great Peace towards which people of good will throughout the centuries have inclined their hearts, of which seers and poets for countless generations have expressed their vision, and for which from age to age the sacred scriptures of mankind have constantly held the promise, is now at long last within the reach of the nations."

It then holds out the choice open to mankind, peace through "unimaginable horrors" due to the continuation of current values and behavior or peace now " . . . by an act of consultative will. . . . " The letter concludes with a momentous challenge to the rulers and kings of the earth to respond to the call of Bahá'u'lláh for a global convocation of those leaders to " . . . consider such ways and means as will lay the foundations of the world's Great Peace amongst men." The Universal House of Justice suggests the United Nations as convenor and asks every human being to " . . . lift up their voices in willing assent."

Can there be any activity more relevant, exciting and "peace-full" than to urge your family, friends, colleagues, local and national leaders, indeed, everyone you meet to raise their voices to request that this meeting be held? Those who have wondered what they can do for peace no longer need have any doubt or hesitation. Let our lives be a mirror of the fulfilled opportunities of our incredible age. Peace.

When I die, my deeds will follow along with me—that is how I imagine it. I will bring with me what I have done. In the meantime it is important to ensure that I do not stand at the end with empty hands.

Carl Jung
Memories, Dreams, Reflections

Notes

This essay is dedicated to Ashley Mae Phillips, born October 6, 1985.

1. *Gleanings from the Writings of Bahá'u'lláh* (Wilmette, Ill.: Bahá'í Publishing Trust, 1939) p. 255.
2. E. Lazlo, *A Strategy for the Future* (New York: George Braziller, 1974) p. vii.
3. Shoghi Effendi, *The World Order of Bahá'u'lláh* (Wilmette, Ill.: Bahá'í Publishing Trust, 1938) p. 190.
4. Shoghi Effendi, quoted in *Lights of Guidance* (New Delhi: Bahá'í Publishing Trust, 1983) pp. 92–93.
5. *Gleanings*, p. 250; Browne, *A Traveller's Narrative*, p. xl.
6. The Universal House of Justice, *Wellspring of Guidance* (Wilmette, Ill.: Bahá'í Publishing Trust, 1969) p. 109.
7. The Universal House of Justice, quoted in *Lights of Guidance*, pp. 90–91.
8. E. F. Schumaker, *Small Is Beautiful* (New York: Harper & Row, 1973) p. 21.
9. *Selections from the Writings of 'Abdu'l-Bahá* (Haifa: Bahá'í World Centre, 1978) p. 282.
10. *Tablets of Bahá'u'lláh* (Haifa: Bahá'í World Centre, 1978) p. 90.
11. Marilyn Ferguson, *The Aquarian Conspiracy* (Los Angeles: J.P. Tarcher, Inc., 1980) p. 323.

12. 'Abdu'l-Bahá, *The Secret of Divine Civilization* (Wilmette, Ill.: Bahá'í Publishing Trust, 1957) p. 103.

13. 'Abdu'l-Bahá, quoted in *The Divine Art of Living* (New York: Brentano's, 1926) p. 163.

14. Rudolph Ballentine, M.D., *Diet and Nutrition* (Honesdale, Penn.: Himalayan International Institute, 1978) p. 4.

15. Quoted in *Lights of Guidance*, pp. 1–2.

16. Shoghi Effendi, *The World Order of Bahá'u'lláh*, p. 9.

17. The Universal House of Justice, *Wellspring of Guidance*, p. 31.

The Global Agenda

by Charles O. Lerche

> *Are not these intermittent crises that convulse present-day society due primarily to the lamentable inability of the world's recognized leaders to read aright the signs of the times, to rid themselves once for all of their preconceived ideas and fettering creeds, and to reshape the machinery of their respective governments according to those standards that are implicit in Bahá'u'lláh's supreme declaration of the Oneness of Mankind...* [1]

> *... the traditional agenda of international affairs—the balance among major powers, the security of nations—no longer defines our perils or our possibilities... Now we are entering a new era. Old international patterns are crumbling: old slogans are uninstructive; old solutions are unavailing. The world has become interdependent in economics, in communications, in human aspirations.* [2]

IT IS A TRUISM, if not a cliche, to state that we live in a world of multiple crises. But this is, nevertheless, an accurate description of humanity's present condition. The two quotations above reflect, in different ways, the perception of humankind's emergence from a global socio-political life marked by competitive plurality into a new, complicated, and rather dangerous condition of global interdependence. Written over fifty years ago, the first passage, from the essay "The Goal of a New World Order" by the Guardian of the Bahá'í Faith, Shoghi Effendi, attributes the crises of our time to a lack of adequate response from leaders to the realities of interdependence—realities which demand the eventual unification of all salient aspects of planetary life. The second passage, written only ten years ago, is from a speech by one of the foremost figures in both the theory and practice of American foreign policy, Henry Kissinger. Though still very much an upholder of the classical approach to international politics, Kissinger has yet been compelled by the changing environment of foreign policy formulation and execution to acknowledge that what he calls the "traditional agenda" of foreign policy is no longer comprehensive and to admit that some sort of new approach is required.

The literature of the Bahá'í Faith, as witnessed by the above quotation, portrays our present troubled time as a necessary period of transition before a much brighter and more orderly future. The outstanding characteristic of this transition is the growing awareness of and commitment to worldwide human solidarity: the emergence of and affective committment to a global, supranational, community of man. As of 1985, no one could pretend that this goal had been reached; but this author would submit that we are closer than most would suspect, that the crises which define our age are all indicative of one macro-evolutionary turning point for our species. Either we must forge effective patterns of international cooperation and create just means of peaceful conflict resolution, or we run the risk of extinction.[3] Thus, we live in extraordinary times.

From this perspective then, the fact that Henry Kissinger and others like him[4] have come to acknowledge the changing nature of the international system is a hopeful sign.[5] But, we might wish to examine what it is about the present global agenda that differs so radically from what conservative statesmen and analysts of world affairs have come to regard as status quo. This paper will discuss that question. Our theme is that each of the issues on the world's current agenda is, in fact, a reason for swifter progress toward a new world order based on the principle of the oneness of humankind.

Before we can analyze the global agenda we must decide what it is. This is not as straightforward as it may seem: the world appears vastly different from different viewpoints. One method of establishing a list of major world concerns might be to survey the topics of debate at the United Nations, or to analyze the content of major speeches by world leaders, noting which issues are most often mentioned or which receive the most emphasis. Another more readily executed approach is to rely on the judgment of experts, in this case scholars of international relations. One textbook on world politics provides the following headings: war and arms control; ideology and nationalism; technology and the ecosystem; North-South relations and development; multinational corporations; ethnic nations and terrorist groups; and human rights.[6] Though lists by other experts may vary a bit or define the areas differently, few would dispute that these are topics central to the concerns of all governments and peoples and are issues often treated in international arenas. Therefore, we will briefly summarize important aspects of each topic and demonstrate that any meaningful solution to the problems posed requires a more integrated global society than now exists.

War and Arms Control. For many people the problems of war and arms control head the global agenda. Certainly this area of concern provides clear evidence of how the world has evolved beyond the classical norms of interstate behavior.[7] In the past, war was considered a normal part of foreign policy: states went to war when an important objective, as defined by the national interest, could be achieved through no other tool of statecraft. The famous maxim of Clausewitz that "war is politics carried on by other means" sums up the classical position. From 1914, however, this situation began to change. Now war has become a threat to the very existence of that same international system in which formerly it was a standard tool of statecraft. How did this happen?

Generally speaking, there are two reasons. First, weapons of all kinds, most particularly nuclear weapons, have become so destructive as to make any full-scale conflict, not a war of limited objectives, but a war of annihilation (at least potentially). Second, incompatible ideologies, whether secular or religious, tend to exacerbate international conflicts to the level of total wars intended to achieve complete domination over the enemy. Given these two factors, both of which play a part in the East-West conflict for example, the major contemporary powers have at various times shown interest in limiting the competition for armaments which accompanies their political rivalry. Though arms control talks have stalled recently, the peoples of the N.A.T.O. countries in Europe have shown increasing anxiety over the continued arms race and the recent deployments of missiles in Western and later Eastern Europe. There has been serious talk in the Congress of the United States of "freezing" America's production of nuclear arms, and more extreme elements have advocated unilateral nuclear disarmament.

The above sketch, brief as it is, raises the question of *why*. If all now acknowledge that a major global nuclear war cannot be meaningfully won, and that a world without nuclear weapons is highly desirable, *why* does the arms race continue unabated? Leaving aside for the moment the question of vested interests in arms production, one answer is simply that two, or more, powerful opponents are not able to trust each other sufficiently to carry out whatever disarmament or arms control agreements might be formulated.[8]

Advocates of disarmament, such as Clark and Sohn,[9] have

specified elaborate procedures for monitoring all stages of the process; and they would give authority to carry out such a task to a greatly strengthened United Nations organization. They maintain that the task of controlling war and arms cannot be effectively accomplished in an international society where power and authority remain so decentralized. Rather, an institution or institutions are required which will protect the peace and integrity of the international community as a whole from the aggression or unwisdom of any of its members.[10] This was the original purpose of the United Nations and the need for it has certainly not decreased in the last forty years.

Though in the past states sought security through armaments, real security in our time lies in disarmament. A vehicle for the exercise of global authority is required to carry out such an unprecedented but necessary step.[11] If war and arms control were the only issue on the global agenda, perhaps a single functional international agency, with extensive inspection powers, would be sufficient. But, as we will see below, arms are not the only issue which may require this sort of treatment.

Ideology and Nationalism. Much has been written about ideology and nationalism and their roles in international relations.[12] But what concerns us here are these basic questions: to what do people owe their highest allegiance? and, what concepts and values define the world in which they live? The nation-state is the object of most people's strongest feelings of loyalty, and many countries, as political scientist Hans Morgenthau has explained,[13] either overtly or tacitly articulate and promote some system of values which their citizens are expected to adopt and support. The multiplicity of nation-states—each of which demands total loyalty from its citizens—and the variety of ideological systems—many of which are mutually incompatible (i.e., capitalist vs. communist, or materialist vs. religious)—find themselves, not suprisingly, in competition and conflict. Again, the confrontation between the Warsaw Pact and N.A.T.O. is the example *par excellence* of what ideological conflict in our technologically advanced age can mean.

The influence of ideology and nationalism on a people's assessment of their prospects and priorities should not be underestimated. The United Nations Educational, Scientific, and Cultural Organization (UNESCO) is founded on the premise that "war begins in the minds of men." It would seem that humanity is severely divided by limited concepts. Yet the objective fact remains that we are a single planetary species facing a single set of planetary problems. This reality is dramatically underlined by photographs of the earth taken from space. Astronauts report that they can see no national boundaries.[14] Thus, the current global conflict of disparate value systems is hindering the minds of men, so to speak, from coming to terms with the reality of an interdependent world.

Since the impulse to national and ideological commitment is deeply rooted in human beings, and is necessary to social integration, it would be unreasonable to propose it be abandoned. Instead, it must be reforged to foster rather than frustrate increasingly close interaction among the peoples of the world. A number of avenues to achieve this end have been suggested in recent years. One, put forward by the scholars associated with the Institute for World Order,[15] is called "global humanism."[16] It is secular in orientation and centers on a set of four values believed to be essential to human material well-being and, thus, to a positive global future.[17] The promotion of these values can be used as a yardstick by which institutions and policies may be judged and evaluated as either advancing or acting counter to "human," as opposed to "national" interests.

When we turn to the issue of religion, we must acknowledge that ideologies based on religious fanaticism are extremely difficult to change. They often exercise total mental and emotional control over their adherents; and for just this reason they can foster, or abet, destructive and vicious conflict—of which there are, unfortunately, multiple examples in our time. We suggest that to remain relevant to mankind's present needs religion must develop a sense of "global spirituality" to replace narrow sectarian and doctrinal disputes. The basis for such an attitude could be found in the understanding that humanity, in all its diversity, is the creation of one ultimate Source of Being. This Supreme Creator has been called by different names in different religious communities, but in fact is similar in each of them.

Such an evolution of perspective among the followers of the various religions would further entail a conscious turning away from differences toward shared views and concerns. Some will feel that this is asking too much of what are, generally, tradition-bound institutions. However, Bahá'ís and others[18] feel that the spirit of the age requires such a forward step in man's thinking. Only in this way can the intensity of religious conviction be channeled into the service of a new global order such as the one we have suggested. A well-known political scientist, Arnold Wolfers,[19] has pointed out that effective international cooperation depends on a sense of affinity between peoples and governments. An emphasis on "global spirituality," as well as "global humanism" could assist greatly in fostering this requisite affinity.

Technology and the Ecosystem. The package of bedeviling issues pertaining to environmental quality provides perhaps the single clearest example of how the present competitive nation-state system must either evolve effective community-wide institutions or suffer the consequences of a deteriorating condition. The biosphere, after all, does not reflect national boundaries. When man, and his technology, interacts with the biosphere, the effects may not remain localized within the boundaries of the state where the interaction was initiated. Oil spills, acid rain, and fall-out from atmospheric nuclear tests (now, fortunately, uncommon) are good examples of this problem. Such events tend to undermine the foundations of the idea of national sovereignty: that states are, by definition, geographically isolated and independent of each other in all essential aspects of their national lives.

Humanity's highly developed technological capacity thus raises a multitude of questions about the future. Every technology has effects on man and his environment. We have learned through bitter experience that even apparently benevolent or harmless technologies may have unforeseen negative consequences. Who would have guessed that aerosol sprays could wreak dangerous havoc on the environment? But, a few years ago it was observed that the accumulation of fluorinated hydrocarbons (released from the sprays) in the upper atmosphere was diminishing the level of ozone there; and ozone forms an essential shield to the earth from dangerous solar rays and helps maintain a steady global temperature. Examples of this kind are far too numerous to list. They strongly suggest that there may be more, as yet undiscovered, negative side effects of so-called technological breakthroughs.

This is not to suggest that humanity should retreat to a technologically backward way of life so as to avoid befouling the planet through careless innovation. Rather, we should acknowledge that the whole of the earth's environment must be treated with equal care and respect by all governments, private organizations, and individuals. This broader concern could only be meaningfully addressed by the establishment of a world environmental authority, perhaps also within the context of a stronger United Nations, which could arrest ecological decay whoever or whatever the cause.

Some contemporary thinkers see an important connection

between this issue of environmental quality and the need for a global spirituality.[20] They maintain that a responsible global ecological policy is part of man's responsibility as the most intelligent species on the earth, the one to whom dominion over all other species has been given by a benevolent if fundamentally inscrutable Providence. They believe we humans must realize that we are accountable for what we do to the earth. The global humanist, on the other hand, would say that whatever our "cosmic" responsibilities may be, we should at least be cautioned to ecological sanity by a commitment to the welfare of our children, and their children, whose quality of life will be greatly affected by the decisions made, or not made, in the next few years. Though Robert Heilbroner, the economist, has posed the rhetorical question: "What has posterity ever done for me?"[21] this author believes that few people are yet so supremely selfish as to consciously deprive future generations of their opportunity to live in a healthy environment. The affirmative direction, therefore, lies in educating an ever increasing proportion of mankind to the reality of ecological decay and the imperative need for a global effort to combat it.

North-South Relations and Development. The United Nations has proclaimed two consecutive decades of development which, according to most assessments, have been failures.[22] The least developed countries (particularly those in Africa), the so-called "Fourth World," are facing *absolute* levels of development below what they enjoyed in earlier periods. As a result, relations between the formerly colonial Western countries with market economies—the "North"—and the "developing" countries in general—the "South"—have never been worse. In fact during the 1970s the North-South confrontation replaced the East-West confrontation (then enjoying a period of short-lived detente) as the central concern of the international community.

That prospects of real economic growth in all but a few

of the Southern countries are severely limited by technological dependence, educational backwardness, dependence on a few agricultural exports exchanged under poor terms of trade, severe debt burdens, public officials linked to the interests of foreign capital, etc., is well known and outlined in detail elsewhere.[23] The lack of substantial progress in the much publicized debate over the so-called New International Economic Order is instructive in this regard. The South employs rhetoric heavily laden with moral condemnation of the North for its imperialism which had the effect of integrating the Southern countries into the global economy in a peripheral and dependent position, and demands that the structure of global economic relations be modified to treat poorer countries more equitably.[24]

An ironic aspect of this confrontation is that, in fact, the Northern countries are just as dependent on the Southern countries as the South is on them. If the majority of Third World economies stagnate or deteriorate, who will buy the industrial exports of the developed countries? Nobody really benefits from widespread global poverty or from a global economic structure which prevents all but a few poorer economies from escaping the vicious cycle of their poverty. Here we have another no-win situation similar to nuclear confrontation and ecological depletion—and yet humankind does not seem to know how to break the deadlock.

Humanity's fragmented sense of identity may well be at the root of the issue. Certainly few national decision-making elites could afford to feel complacent if as substantial a proportion of their fellow countrymen were faring as badly in a national economic system as are poverty-stricken masses of the world in the global economy. However, since to many of the wealthy, the people most seriously affected are "foreigners" who perhaps look different and speak strange languages and are, according to the logic of the state system, even potential enemies, the people of the North (or at least some of them) may find the South's plight less compelling and really not fundamentally their problem. Assuming that enough resources, in terms of technology and raw materials, exist to make some notable improvement in the condition of the masses of world poor, we can only conclude that humanity's sense of solidarity and world community has not evolved far enough to provide an affective climate in which the North-South confrontation can be resolved.

This author doubts if anything short of a real humanitarian effort channeled through an international organization, rather than some sort of bargain worked out according to the canons of economic "rationality," holds any hope of progress. Why, according to standard economic reasoning, should the North give up its dominant position which brings such enormous short-term benefits and contributes to national prestige? Clearly its representatives will not consider such a course, even though, as we pointed out above, it would serve them in the longer run. Action guided by enlightened self-interest is rare in public affairs. Various special interest groups in the developed countries inhibit their leaders from adopting long-term policies that might take account of conditions of global interdependence. So far, national interest has taken precedence over human or global interest in the North-South dialogue. Until this is changed, the confrontation will persist and is likely to become more volatile.

Multinational Corporations. The economic life of modern man, the production and distribution of goods and services, has reached levels of volume and complexity difficult to imagine and the principal agent of planetary commercial life has become the multinational corporation (MNC). The MNC is defined simply as a business enterprise that operates in more than one country. What attracts our attention, however, are the few hundred firms that dominate global output. They have concentrated economic power to such an extent that the annual earnings of General Motors Corporation, for instance, exceed the gross national products of all but about forty nation-states. Also, the geographical spread of the MNC combined with its flexibility and its ability to move capital from one country of operation to another make it extremely difficult to monitor by any one host state.

One need only consider the role major oil companies have played in the matrix of Middle East politics to get some idea of the part MNCs play in international relations. As Lerche and Said have stated:

> The patterns of investment and activity of these corporations affect issues of war and peace, intervention and nonintervention, and may even determine the long-term prospects for world economic development.[25]

The MNC uses modern technology and managerial skills to pursue private ends, and the international system of separate sovereignties cannot control it. Rather, the MNC uses the international anarchy of the state system to its own advantage. To date, the United Nations though recognizing the dangers of allowing such powerful economic units to remain unaccountable to anyone but their own boards of directors has been unable to establish a meaningful code of conduct to regulate these corporations.

What is to be done? Are economic giants which largely control the material life of all of the Western industrialized countries, most of the developing world, and even certain key aspects of the socialist economies to be allowed to pursue their ends without any restraints to protect the interests of mankind? Here again is a situation which would be deemed intolerable at the national level, even in the most laissez-faire of economies, but which cannot yet be prevented in the international community. However, unless the United Nations or some other body is endowed with the power and authority to change the present status quo the answer to the question above is yes. It should be mentioned that statesmen and scholars recognize the anomaly of this situation. Various approaches are under consideration to correct it. Still, a complete solution may well require the erection of new and original world economic institutions. Only these could insure a climate of equity and stability in business from which all, including the MNCs, would benefit.

Ethnic Nations and Terrorist Groups. These are two separate but related issues. First, we have the problem of subnational, ethnically homogenous groups which demand more autonomy—either within a nation-state, or through the formation of their own state. The Basques in Spain and France are one prominent example, and the Kurds in Iraq, Iran and Turkey are another. In this regard we encounter a peculiarity of the current global order: the multination state. When minority, ethnic nations are mistreated within a country—or feel that they have been—they will be inclined to rebel against the authority of the state, which they see as being dominated by rival ethnic interests. This occurred in Nigeria, for example, during the events which led up to the Biafran secession. A well integrated ethnic group which is largely confined to one definable section of territory provides a formidable base for a violent uprising. The more acute their sense of injustice, the more violent their struggle (providing, of course, they have a minimum of means). If the group finds itself in more than one state, like the Basques and the Kurds, the confusion generated by its agitation can have very widespread effects indeed.

How is such an issue to be treated under the classical rules of international law? Not at all, since ethnic nations are subnational units and as such have no status in international law. However, there are often important international linkages between ethnic separatists and foreign states, or the agents of foreign states. Thus, the rules of international law are, in this case, behind the realities of international behavior. What is lacking is a world system for the articulation and adjudication (or arbitration) of grievances through which potential separatist groups might express their complaints and from which they might hope to receive justice. If such tribunals existed, there would be less need, and certainly less support, for violent uprisings by ethnic minorities.

Terrorism, as a class of political acts, is often used by ethnic groups in their struggles. As sympathetic as one may be toward a group's goals, terrorism itself must be condemned. Thus, the issue to be considered is how can such terrorism be controlled and ultimately eliminated. One step, as mentioned above, is by providing access to peaceful and just means of conflict settlement. Another would be uniform, global laws against terrorists. Though the world community is working toward more cooperation against terrorism, unless the cooperation is universal, terrorists will, in theory at least, always have some potential sanctuary and the system of prevention and control will not be able to provide the needed security for international intercourse. Furthermore, such a system would require that states refuse to assist or harbor terrorists even though their ideology may be very similar to the state's own. In other words, states must sacrifice partisan commitments for the communitywide value of freedom from terrorism. Thus, short of a global police force, the control of terrorism requires a one hundred percent commitment by all states to stop the *act* of terrorism regardless of who commits it. The headlines tell us that such a degree of normative consensus has not yet been achieved, but there are some signs at least that it could eventually be realized.[26]

Human Rights. When we come to human rights, our last area of concern, we face two fundamental issues: what are the basic human rights, and who should insure that these rights are enjoyed by everyone? The notion of human rights is problematic to begin with. Though there is some consensus that every human being is due some rights to insure a minimum level of existence worthy of his dignity as a person, various cultures have conceived these rights in different ways. At the moment, a conception derived from the Western liberal tradition and from Socialist thinking (also Western for that matter) have found expression in formal United Nations documents on human rights.[27] However, the Islamic world has a very different conception of the rights of the individual, as do even more ancient cultural systems. This cultural-normative heterogeneity has led Adda Bozeman, a student of culture, politics, and history, to conclude that under such conditions meaningful world law is not possible.[28] We can deduce from her argument that it might also be impossible to list a set of human rights acceptable to all. Of course, while the Western countries were economically and politically dominant, their cultures and their legal systems were imitated in many weaker and poorer societies. However, this is not a firm enough basis for such a far-reaching idea as a global bill of human rights. There is, after all, no world constitution of which a list of human rights might form a part, and in the context of which such a list would seem more meaningful.

Which brings us to the second issue. Basic human rights, as defined by the United Nations, are violated constantly and little can be done but to document and publicize the abuses and hope world public opinion (that most nebulous of forces) can restrain the violators. What, one may ask, is served by formulating schema of rights which cannot be guaranteed and against the violation of which there is no channel of redress in many countries?[29]

If the world community's efforts to provide human rights—political, social, and economic—to all are sincere (admittedly an open question), it is very hard to imagine their fulfillment without world institutions to guarantee free exercise of those rights. What machinery this might entail is not, perhaps, as important as the realization that little can be achieved in a world of separate legal communities. Even if a few major states adopt the promotion of human rights as an important goal of foreign policy, as did the Carter Administration in the United States, only very limited progress can be made. In other words, there can be no universal human rights without a universal human community with communitywide norms and a world legal order integrated to provide for the free exercise of those rights. What has happened in the area of human rights so far at the world level represents a preliminary effort to come to grips with the issues, but further thought and experimentation is necessary before the concept becomes meaningful to a majority of mankind.

We have covered in a general way a set of global issues. But it should be understood that this is only a subset of the whole which emphasizes more tangible and topical problems. Obvious omissions include such areas as alienation, social breakdown, prejudice, and the erosion of moral values. But these, it could be argued, would be found on a rather different sort of global agenda. Our purpose has been to demonstrate that the world macrocrisis has brought out the acute need for: (1) a greatly increased sense of human solidarity, or international affinity, and (2) adequate global institutions to deal with those problems that cannot be solved by states working in isolation.[30]

There is no such thing as state autonomy and it is not rational to pretend that autonomy is a reasonable goal of state policy. Unless checked, the human race itself could be a sacrifice to the pursuit of such an anachronistic ideal. A vision of interdependence, and later oneness, would provide a much better working basis for state interaction. It is just such a perspective that is struggling to emerge amidst the crises of our time.

The Bahá'í community and other world-minded groups[31]

are making sincere efforts to assist humanity in passing this evolutionary threshold. Education is a primary tool for this effort since it has become imperative that old stereotypes and outmoded conceptions be challenged with contradictory data such as that presented here. Perhaps then the rudiments of world-mindedness can be grasped. Of course, a far-reaching, coordinated effort could produce a whole new generation of children who grow up thinking and acting as world citizens, and materials for this kind of pedagogy are being developed.

Thus, there is a basis for hope. There is something one can do in the face of the numbing immensity of the contemporary human predicament. Bahá'ís, at least, are sure that the present difficult period will eventually give way to an epoch of human unity and fulfillment which is too glorious to imagine. That time will either be brought nearer or delayed by the response humanity makes to the issues we have raised. All human beings must, ultimately, face the need for personal and social transformation summarized in this brief quotation from the Bahá'í Scriptures: *"Let your vision be world embracing, rather than confined to your own self."*[32]

Notes

This is a revised version of a paper presented at the first seminar sponsored by the West African Centre for Bahá'í Studies, November 12, 1984, at the University of Ife, Ile Ife, Nigeria.

1. Shoghi Effendi, "The Goal of a New World Order" in *The World Order of Bahá'u'lláh* (Wilmette, Ill.: Bahá'í Publishing Trust, 1938) p. 36.

2. "A New National Partnership," speech by Secretary of State Henry A. Kissinger, Los Angeles, January 24, 1975. News release, Dept. of State, Bureau of Public Affairs, Office of Media Services, p. 1.

3. Literature describing the crises is vast, but a good introduction is Falk, Richard A., *This Endangered Planet* (New York: Vintage Books, 1972).

4. See Dolman, A. J., *Resources, Regimes, World Order* (New York: Pergamon Press, 1981) chapters 1 and 2, for other examples.

5. The author is being only guardedly optimistic.

6. Lerche, C. O. (Jr.) and Said, A. A., *Concepts of International Politics* (Englewood Cliffs, N.J.: Prentice-Hall, 1979). The first author listed here is this author's father.

7. By the classical norms is meant the notion of "power politics."

8. Here we are assuming that the powers concerned would negotiate in good faith, which is clearly not always the case.

9. Clark, Grenville and Sohn, Louis B., *World Peace Through World Law* (Cambridge, Mass.: Harvard University Press, 1962).

10. The exact makeup of the institutions does not concern us, though the author is aware that their formulation would be a highly complex task.

11. The interested reader is referred to Thee, Marek (ed.), *Armaments, Arms Control and Disarmament* (Paris: UNESCO, 1981).

12. See, among others, Ebenstein, William, *Today's Isms: Communism, Fascism, Capitalism, Socialism*, 7th ed. (Englewood Cliffs, N.J.: Prentice-Hall, 1973).

13. Morgenthau, Hans J., *Politics Among Nations* (New York: Alfred A. Knopf, 1967) chapter 7.

14. Here we refer to the so-called "Vision of Apollo."

15. See Mendlovitz, Saul H., *On the Creation of a Just World Order* (New York: The Free Press, 1975).

16. See Johansen, Robert C., *The National Interest and the Human Interest* (Princeton, N.J.: Princeton University Press, 1980) chapters 1 and 2.

17. The values most often mentioned are (1) The minimization of large scale collective violence, (2) the maximization of social and economic well-being, (3) the realization of fundamental human rights and of conditions of political justice, and (4) the maintenance and rehabilitation of ecological quality.

18. Global Education Associates, who publish the Whole Earth Papers are another example of an organization promoting global spirituality. See paper no. 16: "Spirituality and World Order."

19. Wolfers, Arnold, *Discord and Collaboration: Essays on International Politics* (Baltimore: Johns Hopkins Press, 1962).

20. The work of Thomas Berry, Associate Professor of History of Religion at Fordham University, and other followers of Teilhard de Chardin, exemplify this viewpoint.

21. Heilbroner, Robert L., *An Inquiry into the Human Prospect* (New York: Norton, 1980) postscript page 179.

22. This is clearly brought out in, The Brandt Commission, *North-South* (Cambridge, Mass.: M.I.T. Press, 1981).

23. Brandt Commission, *North-South*.

24. There is a great deal of literature on this situation. A popular introduction is Amin, Samir, *Accumulation on a World Scale*, 2 vols. (New York, 1974).

25. Lerche and Said, *Concepts of International Politics*, p. 258.

26. The policy of Cuba in recent years is instructive in this regard.

27. Here we are referring to the Universal Declaration of Human Rights (1948) and two covenants: one on economic, social, and cultural rights and the other on civil and political rights (1966).

28. Bozeman, Adda A., *The Future of Law in a Multicultural World* (Princeton, N.J.: Princeton University Press, 1971).

29. The European Court of Human Rights is an exception to this general situation.

30. Though we have not dwelt on the specifics of world organization, it should be stated that there are two basic approaches: (1) a consolidated world superstate, probably employing a federal structure; and (2) a system of functional world authorities dealing with specific issue areas such as arms, the environment, development, etc.

31. Two examples of other groups would be the World Federalists and Planetary Citizens.

32. Bahá'u'lláh, *Gleanings from the Writings of Bahá'u'lláh* (Wilmette, Ill.: Bahá'í Publishing Trust, 1939) p. 94.

Human Rights and World Peace

by Tahmineh Roshanian

THE MAIN CONCERN OF CIVILIZATION at the present time is maintaining peace—avoiding wars and other major conflicts on this planet. This will probably continue to be a major issue for coming generations as well. In the present world, nations can no longer expect to be isolated from war or independent of the global system of international relations. Political and economic interdependence among all nations is a fact of our time. This is especially true because of the increasing number of countries that have developed a nuclear capacity and the ever-growing danger of nuclear war. Such a war no longer simply raises the tragic prospect of man-to-man fighting, but promises a war of technology, using ever-advancing destructive scientific weapons, that would spell the end of our civilization.

As international relations has become more complex, the economic interdependence of nations has grown tighter. Social problems within nations and disagreements among nations have multiplied, giving rise to social unrest and national wars. But, the more nations disagree, the more they disrespect one another, the more they ignore one another's rights, the closer the world moves toward the time when there will be no alternative to nuclear war.

A worldwide, lasting peace cannot be achieved without respect for individuals and respect for the groups that they form. Respect for human rights within each country promotes respect for human rights worldwide. Safeguarding the well-being of all nationals depends on the observance of the international laws of human rights within individual states. The behavior of each government toward its own citizens, as well as toward citizens of other countries, therefore, concerns the whole international community. This concern is not temporary, it is permanent and growing.

To ensure that human rights are respected and practiced in all countries, we need strong international institutions that will monitor governments and will have the power to intervene in cases of violations. At the same time, we need to educate ourselves and our children about international human rights and make them a moral priority.

Several institutions, governmental and non-governmental, exist today as a result of the enormous number of violations of human rights perpetrated in this century. In fact, never before in history have we had such a level of abuse of human rights in the world. Existing institutions have been unable to control and correct human rights violations effectively. In practice, all states violate human rights, and no effective force has been able to stop them. There have been occasions when a particular government has been forced to correct its behavior and stop its violations of human rights. But these cases are rare.

The basic questions of the human rights debate are: (1) whether the way a particular government treats its own citizens is or should be a matter of international concern; (2) whether efforts by one nation to change the human rights policies of other nations should be broadly accepted as permissible, as legitimate exercises of influence in international relations, or as constituting improper interference in other nations' internal affairs; (3) whether it is possible to reach agreement on a meaningful human rights rule to correct violations; (4) whether governments can in practice be expected to support international human rights efforts; (5) whether international concern for human rights can really hope to affect a state's behavior toward its own citizens, or assist in solving the problems resulting from violations of human rights; and (6) whether international human rights laws can affect the relationship between nations with regard to their human rights concerns.[1]

It is reasonable to expect that any meaningful international human rights law will address all of these questions and provide some assurance that such rights will be protected. But we are as yet a great distance from achieving these goals. Nevertheless, a number of institutions have been established that have achieved some degree of success. It is our hope that in the future human rights will be customarily respected and upheld by a strong and well-intentioned international institutional body. Nevertheless, we should not forget that institutional reforms in this area can only be a safeguard to protect us from serious problems. What is actually needed are far-reaching reforms in the areas of education, economics, socialization, and personal life. We need to structure a new world order in which respect for human rights will be a basic element of national and international life.

In this quest for a new order, governments will play a crucial role. But prior to this, individuals and nongovernmental groups must work for change. This paper will focus, therefore, on the nongovernmental and noninstitutional changes that might promote respect for human rights and make violations easier to correct. In particular, it will be concerned with the role of education, of the media, of family, religion, and morality. Likewise, it will mention scientific and technological developments, economic and social development, and arms control.

I should caution the reader at the outset that this paper is not perfect, nor is my research on these subjects complete. This essay is only an attempt to highlight some of the most important issues involved in the struggle for justice and human dignity. I hope that this work will open opportunities for research by others in the field of human rights.

The Need for a New World Order. To observe that the world is ill and is troubled by a multitude of social problems is to mouth a cliché. Perhaps the insight that the Bahá'í teachings can bring to this sad state of affairs is the realization that all the various social evils and dilemmas that we face are interrelated. No particular problem can be solved without addressing every other problem. There can be no effective improvement in the present situation unless whole areas of human life change. Specifically, we cannot expect that human rights will be respected and protected by the governments of the world as long as most of them face such threatening economic, social, political, and moral problems. Human rights are violated by governments because they cannot respond to the legitimate demands of their people and satisfy them properly. Therefore, they control discontent and unrest by the use of violence and repression. Human rights violations have their roots in deprivation and human suffering.

The old world order is dying, and our current systems are unable to respond to the new and urgent demands of mankind. As long as the present global situation of competing nationalisms, antagonistic ideologies, imbalance of resources, and international anarchy continues, we cannot expect to effectively implement human rights norms throughout the world. Meanwhile, our capacity for self-destruction is constantly increasing. Starvation, terrorism, genocide, war, civil conflict, revolution, rebellion, poverty, overpopulation, social disorientation, drug abuse—these problems make headlines every day. So far, the world has failed to come up with peaceful solutions to them.

Although human rights violations are the cause of some of these disasters, such violations involve only the shortcomings of governments and are, moreover, related to other problems. The need is for a new, more just world order that will promote an atmosphere of international cooperation, not based on differences, but founded on the mutual interests of mankind—survival and the advancement of all areas of humanity's physical and mental capacities. These interests must include the abolition of war. Violence cannot be used as a means to peace: violence begets violence and leads to further violations of human life and liberty.

There have been many models for a new global system suggested by religious leaders, social scientists, and international lawyers. It is not the purpose of this paper to examine these various models. Rather, our point is that machinery for the enforcement of human rights law is a necessary part of any meaningful vision of a new world order.

We stand at a critical moment in history. The world is on the brink of change or destruction. Whatever changes come must provide for the effective protection of human rights. While the responsibility of governments to bring about such changes is profound, there are also noninstitutional changes that may improve prospects for the implementation of human rights norms. These will be discussed below.

My assumption throughout this paper (by no means assured) is that gradual changes will continue to take place that will lead us to a new global order, that we will not have to suffer another World War and then establish a new order out of the massive and disastrous destruction of a world holocaust. Such changes must take place within a fairly short period of time, however, and during our generation. Otherwise, it may be too late for constructive, gradual, and progressive reforms to be effective.

Media Responsibility and Human Rights Violations. In the current world system, international law is ineffective and underdeveloped in the area of investigation into human rights violations. Authorities and concerned organizations must use to a great extent the reports of private media on human rights violations. The fact-finding bodies of both governmental and nongovernmental organizations use the private media as reliable sources of information and facts.

The responsibility of the media is great in observing and reporting human rights violations, objectively and independently of any political system. It is the task of the media to report any wrongdoing of governments in human rights matters and to inform the rest of the world of such incidents as they take place in any country. Usually, the national media is censored in countries where human rights are violated. Therefore, media outside the country must assist local media in reporting and fact finding. The sense of responsibility among the representatives of the media in inquiring into human rights violations must increase to such a degree that no human rights violation will be committed without it being reported to the international tribunals for condemnation and remedy.

Universal Education and Human Rights. One of the reasons that we have so many social and ethical problems in the world is the fact that the majority of people are uneducated and lack the skills and understanding required to cope with an advancing society. Absence of a thorough, well focused, individualized educational system results in an undereducated world population that fails to recognize its true abilities, talents, capabilities, and thus its rights as well. Masses of people remain under the yokes of repressive systems without exerting any real efforts to raise their social values and ethics, or develop skills which might help them and their nations to advance. If a universal educational system can be created so that every individual receives, not only primary education, but develops his or her mind with expanding capacity to deal with the problems of the world, people would be less inclined to allow repressive action by their governments.

Leonard J. Hippchen and Yong S. Yim, in their book entitled *Terrorism, International Crime and Arms Control,* describe their views of a new educational system:

> Education for a developing mankind must be quite different from what it is today. It is entirely too parochial in view, ideological in conception, and indoctrinated in approach. It needs to be raised to the level of dealing primarily with universal realities—natural and physical sciences, true philosophy, the realities of psychology and individual development, and the realities of a socioeconomic-political order, which can work effectively toward social advancement and peace throughout the world.[2]

The role of a world educational system in developing character and ethical values should be emphasized. The governments of the world not only have to provide universal and obligatory education for everyone as one of the rights of all citizens, but should individualize the training and education of both children and adults to raise their level of social advancement. Children must be taught the value of human life, of personal integrity, of the ethical and moral concern for the world, of respecting the rights of others, and of understanding the meanings of those rights. They should learn about their own rights and liberties, while at the same time they are taught to respect and protect the human rights and liberties of others. This kind of education raises the moral responsibility of individuals to respond to and oppose violations of human rights whenever they encounter them.

If the people of the world are taught about their rights and liberties and are trained to defend them, the efforts of international organizations will be more effective in protecting human rights.

Family. The family is the first and primary institution to foster social behavior of children. The family should be strong and united, so that it can rear children with high social understanding and sound and just character. The family has a responsibility to provide effective guidance and training, as well as physical, social, and spiritual development for children. It must strive for the best possible education for youngsters.

If family structure remains strong and support and love for its members become the basis of everyday life, children can easily learn to love first the members of their own families and then to love their fellow men, to respect one another and to be concerned about others. Thus may develop a high level of loving cooperation and social integration. Therefore, the family unit should be supported and encouraged by national and international institutions, both by economic means and structural training. If this can be achieved, within one or two generations there will be fewer problems in the world and those problems will be easier to solve. People will have been taught from childhood to effectively cooperate with one another and to understand and respect each other's rights.

Social, Scientific, Technological Progress. The rapid development of science and technology in the world today has outstripped the rate of social progress and moral development. Thus we observe that as old methods and forms of human rights violations disappear, new forms of violation emerge. For instance, slavery has effectively been abolished in the modern world. But various forms of economic exploitation have replaced it. Methods of torture provide another example: with scientific progress, more effective forms of physical and psychological abuse are possible. Many of these can be accomplished without leaving any physical evidence that might later be detected.

Social progress must keep pace with scientific and technological advancement if the violation of human rights is to be eliminated. The Working Group on Human Rights, in their "New Aspects of the International Protection of Human Rights" has made some recommendations for more effective protection of humanity in this light. They suggest that the United Nations should give priority to examining scientific and technological developments and their consequences for human rights. They further recommend that the U.N. safeguard human rights by developing proper means for keeping up with technological advances.[3]

The United Nations Advisory Committee on the Application of Science and Technology to Development and the Science Advisory Committee to the Secretary-General, the Working Group advised, should constantly monitor new developments in science to identify those which appear to have an impact on human rights issues. Furthermore, member governments were urged to create special scientific advisory committees for the same purpose.[4]

On a noninstitutional level, the scientific community should be held responsible for reporting any new developments in the field that might endanger human rights. Furthermore, in a world that is rapidly moving toward a new order, we must understand that social and moral progress must keep pace with scientific and technological progress if a world free of human rights abuse is to be created.

Economic and Social Development. One of the major factors contributing to the instability of the world is the economic gap between developed and less developed nations. This imbalance of power and wealth has contributed to endless social problems. One reason that human rights are violated more regularly in the less developed countries is because their governments are unable to satisfy the demands of their people, to provide them with better and higher levels of education, to insure their economic well-being, or foster their social improvement. Unable to meet the legitimate demands of the population, these governments resort to repression in order to remain in power.

The establishment of a just, new global order will require that the most developed countries assist the weaker nations in the areas of science, technology, economics, and social advancement. A balance in the economic and social order will eliminate many of the major threats to human rights in the world. The economic and social development of the whole earth should move in one direction. At present, an unjust economic and social balance exists that causes advancement and progress in one country to result in the weakness and deterioration in another nation. Such a system must be changed.

In a new world order, all nations are to be considered as the units of one global system. The economic and social development of the whole world will move in one progressive direction. An example of such a system is the United States of America. Consider the U.S. Federal Government as the world government, and each state as representative of the different nations of the world. The whole of the United States develops in one direction, and such development has a fairly universal effect. No one state is deprived of innovations in trade, economics, scientific development, or social values. All states enjoy the same opportunity and facility to grow and advance together.

The same approach might be adopted for a new world system in which each nation would be treated as a part of one system, and each treated equally. The various units of the whole might differ in the degree of their progress and development, given their natural resources and wealth, but extreme differences would be eliminated. This would be accomplished through an international exchange of information, capital, and materials and through mutual cooperation and concern.

Arms Control and Disarmament. The recent Global 2000 Report to the President of the United States reported that America alone is spending over $450 billion each year on armaments, while giving only $20 billion in economic aid.[5]

Other countries follow the same pattern, allocating the bulk of their resources to arms, and only a small portion on economic betterment. This trend has two consequences: first, there remains less and less money for economic development. This decreases the standard of living for masses of people, and leads to the rise of human frustration and political desperation. Governments, in turn, increase their violations of human rights to control their citizens. Second, massive quantities of arms lead to an increase in violence, repression, terrorism, civil war, and wars between nations.

The elimination of war, or even a relative reduction in the level of arms spending throughout the world, would free vast resources that could be spent for the development of economic and social conditions. Starvation could easily be eliminated as a problem for mankind through the effective management of the world's resources on an international scale. The fabulous sums of money spent on arms could be turned toward the preservation and elevation of human life.

The first step in the abolition of war is the initiation of arms control and gradual disarmament. Nuclear power, in particular, must be brought under control. Nations should be able to limit the production of arms to the level needed only to preserve internal security. A world army, under the control of an international body, and composed of people of all races, sexes and nationalities might preserve peace on earth. Under such a system, the power of governments to violate human rights would be restricted.

Religion and Morality. Religion throughout history has been one of the most powerful institutions of mankind. The majority of the people of the world have strong religious beliefs. Religious belief and religious practice account for some of the most important activities of humanity. Religion, at its origins, has been a source of enlightenment and has provided mankind with tools to advance its social and spiritual development. Unfortunately, the power of religion has often been misused by religious authorities.

Most human rights that are listed in contemporary international sources were originally asserted and proclaimed in religious texts such as the Old Testament, the New Testament, and the Qur'án. Religious teachings admonished justice, fairness, honesty, assistance to the poor, respect for one's parents, and many other rights and moral obligations. The moral standards of religious teachings regarded certain natural rights of man as God-given rights. The concept of the natural rights of man has, in the twentieth century, gradually evolved into secular international human rights issues.

Although all traditional religions uphold and support the concept of human rights, we still observe serious violations of such rights carried out in the name of religion. However, the actions of specific groups, or of individual religious authorities, cannot be taken as reflecting the true principles of any religion. The misconduct of people acting in the name of a religion should not be mistaken for what the followers of that religion may hold as their highest principles.

Most of the religious organizations in the world have, in this century, expressed their support for human rights on moral grounds. The main issue that relates directly to these religious groups is that of religious freedom and the right to choose one's belief. The World Council of Churches has issued many statements and resolutions and has sponsored conferences on religious freedom. The first Assembly of the Council of Churches, in 1948, made a Declaration on Religious Liberty. The rights asserted in this Declaration are: the right to determine one's own faith and creed; the right to express one's religious beliefs in worship, teaching and practice, and to proclaim the implications of these beliefs in relationship to a social or political community; the right to associate with others and to organize with them for religious purposes; and the right of every religious organization to determine its politics and practices for the accomplishment of its chosen purposes.[6]

The second Assembly of The World Council of Churches, in 1954, produced a report called "The Responsible Society in a World Perspective." It emphasized the following rights: protection from arbitrary arrest or other interference that eliminates human rights; the right to express one's religious, moral, and political convictions; the right to political action to change a government without resorting to violence; the right to association, uncontrolled by the State.

"Human Rights and Christian Responsibility" was a report of consultation held by The Commission of the Churches on International Affairs, in Austria, in 1974. This report declared a set of human rights that had much in common with all the above views. These rights were: a basic human right to live, including survival, and eliminating unjust economic, social, and political aspects in the quality of life; the right to enjoy and maintain a cultural identity, including national self-determination, the rights of minorities, etc.; the right to effective democracy; the right to dissent; the right to personal dignity which involves, for example, condemnation of torture or of protracted imprisonment without trial; the right to choose freely a religion or belief, including freedom to manifest one's religion or belief, in teaching, practice, worship, and observance.[7]

A "Universal Islamic Declaration of Human Rights" was issued in 1981, proclaiming the rights of humans as asserted in the Islamic Scripture. As Salem Azzam stated in the Declaration:

> Human Rights in Islam are firmly rooted in the belief that God, and God alone, is the law giver and the source of all human rights. Due to their divine origin, no ruler, government, assembly or authority can curtail or violate in any

way the human rights conferred by God, nor can they be surrendered.[8]

The rights mentioned in this Declaration are: the right to life; the right to freedom; the right to equality and the prohibition against impermissible discrimination; the right to justice; the right to a fair trial; the right to protection against abuse of power; the right to protection against torture; the right to protection of honor and reputation; the right to asylum; the rights of minorities; the right and obligation to participate in the conduct and management of public affairs; the right to freedom of belief, thought, and speech; the right to freedom of religion; the right of free association; the economic order and the rights ensuing therefrom; the right to protection of the property, status, and dignity of workers; the right to social security; the right to found a family, and related matters; the rights of married women; the right to education; the right to privacy; the right to freedom of movement and residence. The rights assessed in the Islamic Declaration stem from the Qur'án and the Sunna, and are based on Islamic law and its traditional implementation in Islamic countries.

There is a Bahá'í declaration of human obligations and rights made on behalf of the Bahá'í Faith. As one of their basic principles, the Bahá'ís believe in the unity of mankind, which can be achieved only through respect for human rights. Bahá'ís believe in the need to establish a new world order, with the goal of establishing justice and peace for humankind. In the Bahá'í Declaration of Human Obligations and Rights it is asserted that: "The Source of Human Rights is the endowment of qualities, virtues and powers which God has bestowed upon mankind without discrimination of sex, race, creed, or nation."[9] Human rights are defined as "an expression of man's divine endowment given social status by a moral and sovereign body"—a right attains a social status only after it has become accepted as a moral value.[10] Thus, human rights can be established in terms of social status only when people realize that life is a God-given gift and that each person has an obligation to meet responsibilities before God, society, and self.

Among the essential human rights characterizing the new world era promoted by Bahá'ís are those concerned with: the individual; the family; race; work and wealth; education; worship; the social order. These rights constitute the main guideline, and detailed rights are defined in many sources. However, special emphasis is placed on some of the rights that are of concern today and are constantly violated. Of special concern are: the elimination of the crime of genocide through the teaching of the Bahá'í principle of the oneness of mankind; the oneness of religion; loyalty to government; the abolition of war; and the creation of a new world civilization.

On the rights of minorities, a statement was presented by the Bahá'í International Community to the United Nations Seminar on the Promotion and Protection of Human Rights of National, Ethnic and Other Minorities held in Ohrid, Yugoslavia. This statement concerned the rights of minorities and their status in the Bahá'í Faith:

> The Bahá'í International Community is multi-racial, multi-national and multi-lingual. . . . Bahá'ís regard all people as invaluable members of society whose talents and unique contributions as individuals and/or groups, whether in minority or the majority, are equally important factors in building a new world.
> To discriminate against any race, on the ground of its being socially backward, politically immature, or numerically in a minority, is a flagrant violation of the spirit that animates the Faith of Bahá'u'lláh.[11]

Some other Bahá'í statements on human rights made to various United Nations bodies concern: the rights of indigenous populations (including fundamental policy; education; information on educational establishments and institutions;

language; cultural, social and legal institutions; religious rights and practices), the rights of the family, the rights of women (equality of women and men is one of the principles of the religion), the rights of youth, and social and economic justice for all peoples.

A World Religion. True religion can advance both the social and spiritual development of the individual and aid each person to develop a high sense of morality and strong ethical values. Here we do not refer to a once-a-week observance, church attendance, narrow dogma, or to the celebration of religious holidays. Rather, we speak of religion as the highest and most complete expression of the spiritual aspirations of humanity. If children are taught *true* religious values and learn to adopt them in everyday life circumstances, they will develop a sense of morality in all areas of their lives. Again, we emphasize that the simple observance of religious rituals is not enough, and by itself may be an obstacle to the higher goal. True spiritual education and advanced social teachings must be adopted.

Religion offers profound benefits, but also has certain negative aspects. Causes of religious differences and disputes must be eliminated. The limited loyalties of each faith group to its own "one true religion" must be sacrificed for a higher good. Yim and Hippchen, in a discussion of international directions for juvenile justice, write:

> What appears to be needed is a revival of true religious experience within the structure of a world religion, which could reconcile the seeming elements of disunity among the various religions. A unified world religion, incorporating all the people from throughout the world who truly desire to follow the one true God, would represent a powerful influence for social change. These people would need to come from all races, religions, classes, sexes, and nations to be representative. They would need to be

organized into a new structural arrangement that would allow productive spiritual and social growth for all. The worldwide Bahá'í Faith is an example of the kind of institutional structure that would fulfill this role.[12]

Bahá'u'lláh, prophet and founder of the Bahá'í Faith, has written:

That which the Lord hath ordained as the sovereign remedy and mightiest instrument for the healing of all the world is the union of all its peoples in one universal Cause, one common Faith. This can in no wise be achieved except through the power of a skilled, an all-powerful and inspired Physician.[13]

If we truly wish to establish a new world order, with one international government, it will require a unifying power such as a new world religion to accomplish it. Some force is needed that will transform the consciousness of the mass of humanity and challenge the people of all nations to function with a new identity as citizens of the world. The Bahá'ís of the world have long offered their religion as such a force.

Notes

1. Paul Sieghart, *International Law of Human Rights* (Oxford: Clarendo Press; 1983).
2. Young S. Kim and Leonard J. Hippchen, *Terrorism, International Crime, and Arms Control* (Springfield, Ill.: Charles C. Thomas, 1982) p. 264.
3. Luiz B. Sohn and Margaret D. Gayley, "New Aspects of the International Protection of Human Rights," 25th report of the Commission to Study the Organization of Peace, p. 11.
4. Ibid., pp. 11–12.
5. As reported in *Science*, 1980.

6. World Council of Churches, "Religious Freedom, 1948–1975." First Council of Churches.

7. ———, "Main Ecumenical Statements on Principles Concerning Religious Freedom," 1965. Second Council of Churches.

8. Universal Islamic Declaration of Human Rights, September 19, 1981.

9. National Spiritual Assembly of the Bahá'ís of the United States, "A Bahá'í Declaration of Human Rights," 1947.

10. Ibid.

11. Bahá'í International Community, "The Promotion and Protection of Human Rights of National, Ethnic and other Minorities."

12. Young S. Kim and Leonard J. Hippchen, *Terrorism*, p. 263.

13. *Gleanings from the Writings of Bahá'u'lláh* (Wilmette, Ill.: Bahá'í Publishing Trust, 1939) p. 255.

Peace Groups and the Global Pact

by Rouha Rose

IN OCTOBER 1983, sixty-six Bahá'ís in Northwest Washington began to search the Bahá'í Writings for all references to peace, another ten or so were assigned to typing and indexing. One year later, seventy-seven pages, single-spaced, had been found. The most prevalent topic was the role of America in world peace. This effort was not scholarly, nor was it complete. It was, however, an education, affirmation, and inspiration to those involved. Many Bahá'ís, and groups of Bahá'ís, in other places had already begun similar searches.

I had recently resigned a teaching position to assist with family obligations. This allowed a bit of freedom, and in response to Shoghi Effendi's many directives to interact with like-minded groups,[1] I volunteered for the World Without War Council in Seattle at about the same time we began collecting the references on peace. Although I chose this organization accidentally and tentatively, I found I could agree with its objectives: to study and find paths to peace with freedom, and to build bridges between all peoples who share these values. I was comfortable with its methods which utilized the existing system and were constrained by civil obedience.

My first assignment was updating the addresses of all the peace groups in the Seattle area and summarizing the perspective and program of each group. George Weigel, then Director of the Council, now serving as a Fellow at the Woodrow Wilson International Center for Scholars at the Smithsonian Institute in Washington, D.C., had just published *Washington's Window on the World*,[2] a directory of institutions and groups in Washington State which are in one way or another involved in world affairs. I was to talk with those which could be classified as peace groups and also to find groups which had more recently come into being.

All of the fifty-five peace groups in Greater Seattle which I interviewed agreed that war has become intolerably dangerous to mankind.[3] Intolerable is a word that demands action. All of the groups insisted that something must be done. All of them enjoyed and used the freedom to express their views. Although I did not ask the question, I suspect they value that freedom as much as they long for peace.

The thing that differentiates these peace groups from one another seems to be their emotional tone. At one extreme are groups of scholars who make guarded statements and recommendations based on careful research and verifiable data. In the center are many moderate groups that have arisen among religious organizations, women's groups, professional and business organizations (such as the Physicians for Social Responsibility, the Religious Peace Action Coalition of the Church Council, Women's International League for Peace and Freedom, the World Peace Through Law section of the Washington State Bar Association, the World Affairs Council, the American Jewish Committee, etc.). These have a potentially large following with vast resources, and they have counterparts in nations around the world.

The vanguard of the moderate peace groups is not impressive in strength, yet behind it waits the majority of the world's population, exhausted by war, impoverished by high tax burdens, angry and uncertain over the dangers of the future, and eager to get on with life in a new world of justice. The size and the impatience of this force, whose individual members are as yet unaware of their unity, increases as the oppressions and catastrophes daily increase. At the other extreme are groups whose members sound deeply frightened and angry and whose speeches, articles, and activities express that fear.

Although these groups do not yet fully appreciate each other's potential, it seems to me that their common success is enhanced by their differences. The research and action that will lead to lasting peace must be founded on caution and wisdom. Wrong action can be fatal to the planet. But politicians and world leaders, who must initiate the right action, have no time nor inclination to seek, weigh, or even listen to logical argument.

It is the voice of the people, raised higher than all the paid lobbyists and special interest groups, that will attract the attention of the legislators. For example, local attempts to stop Trident submarines with row boats do not stop the submarines now, but they make headlines. This may keep the nation and its leaders focused on the necessity to find the way to peace with freedom. Conservative peace groups are investigating every possibility of attaining world peace and are communicating with legislators continually. If a way is found, it is the urgency of the liberals that will provide the initial thrust, but it is the strength of the center that achieves success.

Another advantage to the diversity of the peace groups is that each freedom-and-peace-loving person can find an association within which he can use his fullest resources.[4] There are groups directed toward conversion from a war machine to a peacetime economy. Others stress the freeze and possible bilateral disarmament. Some spend their resources in fostering person-to-person interaction, such as exchange student and sister-cities programs. Some emphasize the need to bring about peace within the individual, the home, and local community as a foundation for world peace. Others are addressing the environmental issues that have been ignored in the rush of arms technology.

Studies of economics, ecology, conflict resolution, an international auxiliary language, world agriculture, etc., all aim toward the original American dream that the whole world will soon be free: free of war and oppression, whether political, economic, religious, racial; free of malnutrition, disease, illiteracy, etc. All of these freedoms, these human rights, are destroyed by war and cannot be attained as long as the world's resources are dedicated to war. So these peace groups are allies, even though they differ in their perspectives.

In spite of the differences among the peace groups, there seems to be a growing awareness of the need for *unity* in their diversity, if peace is to be achieved. In Washington State, Target Washington is a citizen's organization which assists in organizing networking conferences on the prevention of nuclear war. The Advisory Committee of Target Washington includes the entire Washington congressional delegation. In September, 1985, coinciding with the United Nation's first International Day of Peace, peace groups and leaders of thought met in Olympia to find common goals, increase rapport, add to each other's resources, and assess their combined strength. At the same time, in Seattle, leaders from Target Washington, Physicians for Social Responsibility, World Peace Through Law, Seattle Ecumenical Religious Peace Action Coalition, the World Without War Council, and the Bahá'í community invited some thirty-five leaders to a similar meeting. Both gatherings were well attended, positive in spirit, revealed an existing unity between the groups, and produced promises of mutual assistance, projects, and victory.

In spite of the number and variety of the peace groups, their excellent activities and vigorous networking, as I interviewed the various groups for the World Without War directory, I was surprised to find that none had a plan to attain peace. Activities are based on determination and hope, not on specific objectives designed to abolish war. Those who advocate a freeze on the production of nuclear weapons hope the Soviet leaders will cooperate, but have no evidence that they will. The sentiment they seem to express is that we should take the first serious steps to demonstrate our intentions, whatever their response. I heard no mention of exact steps expected to lead to peace by the proponents of the intellectual approach, although they certainly are seeking them.

Groups speaking for deterrence do not insist that deterrent is a plan for peace. It may buy time, and could even lead to bilateral agreements to reduce contention to a level that does not endanger all life on earth. But negotiations founded on deterrence are not designed to result in peace, but merely to reduce the danger of war. Poison gas is banned but war continues, more horrible day by day. Banning nuclear weapons while allowing deadly conquests to continue is not an outcome favored by any peace groups. So the advocates of a strong deterrent do not disagree that a plan to achieve and maintain peace is needed in addition to deterrence.

Also outside the peace groups is a faction, labeled conservative, which is not opposed to peace, but which values political and civil freedoms above life itself and fears the peace movement may lead to a loss of these freedoms. This element can give its support whenever it is certain that lasting peace and political freedom are not and cannot be mutually exclusive categories. Nor are the wealthy involved in the peace movement relative to their power to effect change. Business must have markets, and the citizens of the whole world are consumers. The present situation of depending on the arms industry and artificially maintaining economic stability, while trying to meet the need abroad through charity, is too expensive, dangerous, unfair, and unwieldy. A plan for peace that safeguards, even extends, freedom, upholds justice, and which allows for free trade must be found.

"The attainment of any object is conditioned upon knowledge, volition and action."[5] There is abundant volition, and motivation can only increase. But because there is no common knowledge of how to initiate peace and halt war, because there is no plan, unified public action is yet impossible.

The Global Pact: How to get from here to peace. About the same time that I became aware through these interviews that peace groups have no specific plan, I was also surprised to discover, in our research on the Bahá'í Writings, a complete, simple, safe, and sure plan designed to achieve international peace. The plan, called "the Pact," was first proposed in 1875, but the communications technology to implement it is just now in place. It was proclaimed to all the peoples of the world in October, 1985, by the international governing body of the Bahá'ís, the Universal House of Justice.

It should be understood that this global pact, although revealed in the Bahá'í Writings, is not a Bahá'í pact. To investigate and support such an agreement is not to investigate and support the Bahá'í Faith, any more than support for the equality of men and women (or any of the principles found in the Bahá'í Writings) is support for the Faith. It would be a detriment if any peace-seeking person or group declined to consider the practicality of the global pact for this reason.

Bahá'ís believe that the following principles are essential to world peace:

the oneness of all races;
the equality of men and women;
universal basic education;
the elimination of prejudice and extremes of wealth and poverty (through profit sharing, social security, income tax, a storehouse form of public assistance, etc.);
the right of and need for individuals to investigate truth independently;

the need to harmonize science and religion;
the protection of cultural differences and of the environment;
the necessity for world government including a tribunal for international consultation;
the need for an international auxiliary language;
the need for all faiths to unify and lead mankind to peace;
the rights of children and other family members;
etc.[6]

All of these speak of the oneness of humanity, of human rights for every individual, of justice. Most of these principles are firmly established in the United States. It may take several generations to bring them into daily individual, family, and social life, but, despite the hue and cry of extremists, the principles themselves are here to stay. In this nation, most have even been formalized into law.

These spiritual principles, which had caused the deaths of more than twenty thousand Bahá'ís in the nineteenth century, which were considered dangerously liberal at the time of World War II, and which are still causing the imprisonment and death of Bahá'ís in Iran, had permeated the minds of the majority of American people by the end of the 1960s. Today all that is left to accomplish is to design a just world order and offer it to the world.

Shoghi Effendi, who led the Bahá'í Faith from 1921 to 1957 writes:

> ... pathetic indeed are the efforts of those leaders of human institutions who, in utter disregard of the spirit of the age, are striving to adjust national processes, suited to the ancient days of self-contained nations, to an age which must either achieve the unity of the world ... or perish.... it behooves the leaders of all the nations ... whether victors or vanquished, ... thoroughly imbued with a sense of world solidarity, ... to carry out

in its entirety the one remedial scheme ... prescribed for an ailing humanity. [He then quotes 'Abdu'l-Bahá, who was speaking to a government official in the United States after sixty years of exile and imprisonment.] You can best serve your country, ... if you strive, in your capacity as a citizen of the world, to assist in the eventual application of the principle of federalism underlying the government of your own country to the relationships now existing between the peoples and nations of the world.[7]

He continues, characterizing the book, *The Secret of Divine Civilization,* as the outstanding contribution of 'Abdu'l-Bahá, to the future reorganization of the world and presents the global pact from that book. It follows in outline form:

The Global Pact

I. *"... a certain number of* [leaders of nations] [who share the same values][8] ... *shall, for the good and happiness of all mankind, ... conclude a binding treaty."*
  A. *"... the frontiers of each and every nation should be clearly fixed,*
  B. *"the principles underlying the relations of governments towards one another definitely laid down,*
  C. *"and all international agreements and obligations ascertained.*
  D. *"... the size of the armaments of every government should be strictly limited ...* [i.e., none need carry a great burden, no member need be a threat to another]
  E. *"... all the governments ... arise to reduce* [any violator] *to ... submission"* [i.e., collective security].
II. *"They* [the certain number that concluded the pact] *must proclaim it to all the world and obtain for it the sanction of all the human race."*[9]

Among the provisions of the pact must be the creation of a tribunal which will arbitrate in cases which might otherwise result in conflict. The candidates for the tribunal must be elected by the parliament or congress of each nation, resulting in a three level selection of tribunal members based on the will of the people.[10] Tribunal consultation and decisions will be a benefit to pact nations. At all levels of human interaction it is inevitable that interests will conflict. Resolving these differences without bloodshed—inexpensively, routinely, promptly, objectively, and fairly—will lift a burden from generations which have lived under the continuous threat of war. In the beginning, if a decision is considered that does not please a member country, the perseverence necessary to work it out will be strengthened by the determination of its citizens to remain safely within the global pact. This is an advantage of taking the pact directly to the people. Treachery, attempts to undermine or abandon the pact, or the tribunal, cannot gain support if the people are their champions. In addition to this bond will be the vulnerability of a nation should it choose to withdraw and survive on only its own resources and defenses. Note the present vulnerability of all small nations to conquest and of all large nations to bankruptcy and blackmail, threats, hostages, terrorism, etc.

Safety is the initial foundation of pact solidarity and stability. When other advantages of membership become tangible—spiritual benefits: with the long-dreamed-of feeling of security, the joy of unity and discovery accompanying open communication and unfettered travel; economic benefits: with free trade of information, resources and skills—these pleasant supports will outweigh the bond of mere mutual survival and the morale of global pact nations will, in addition to being a new life for the people, become a magnet to people outside its protection.

Among the unique aspects of this pact is that it is to be

initiated by and concerned only with friendly nations which respect values of personal freedom, national autonomy, and majority vote. Only nations that wish to follow these principles will be accepted as members. The initiating nations must have no conflict with each other. History has shown there is no lasting gain in treaties put together by opponents. By starting with a nucleus of unified nations, and by adding only those nations committed to its principles, the global pact will be internally sound in its embryonic stage and can grow organically.

Another element that will cement an enduring peace will be fixing national borders. Borders have never been upheld by law. All that is needed for a border to change is a conquest. If the changes that have occurred in the maps of Europe, Asia, and Africa were speeded up, the picture would look like an oil slick on a wind-blown puddle. Families, languages, and religions can be traced many generations, but in some places almost every generation has had to swear loyalty to a different nation in order to survive. The global covenant, by setting borders and negotiating them as each nation joins, will provide legitimacy and stability to nations. This does not mean borders may not be changed for logical and just reasons. Rather, the means of change would be consultation instead of war.

The purpose of this pact differs from those of treaties heretofore. Its establishment and maintenance is for the happiness and good of humankind. The purpose of alliances such as NATO, the OAS, etc., are limited to the well-being of certain nations, political parties, or groups. They have not been able to catch up with crises, let alone move into the work of crisis prevention and creative interaction.

The United Nations (which the Pact complements), although making great contributions in some fields, cannot secure the safety of its members because there is no unity of conscience in its design or in the implementation of its decisions. When decisions are made that benefit only one side of an argument, whether by means of war or majority vote, the results are superficial and temporary. Enemies are made; the loser lives to fight again; the ink is not dry before arms must be stockpiled for the next confrontation. For lasting results, the good and happiness of all people must be sought by the members of the global pact and its tribunal in the resolution of every conflict.

The pact would immediately lessen tensions worldwide because disagreement between member nations themselves could not reach the stage of conflict. Its provisions would provide to these nations an arena for creative, efficient, mutual progress. Serious stress would only occur if a pact nation were attacked by a nation outside the group, but the sanctions that the pact could impose, especially as it became larger, would be such as no nation could afford to ignore.

Consider the value of such a pact to Canada and the United States. Fishing disputes are an example. Many issues have been settled between the two great neighbors without war. However, because there is no established council or tribunal for consultation, when need for problem-solving arises, public debate must reach an embarrassing and demoralizing pitch before legislators give the necessary attention. This is inefficient and even divisive because it tends to pit people against people, instead of using wisdom to meet needs and interests.

Another example of the benefit of a system for consultation and arbitration are the United States themselves. Had each state remained a totally isolated nation as was the wish in the beginning, each with its own military, its own alliances abroad, with differing languages, etc., the wars and competition of the rest of the world would have occurred among states, and our wealth would have been leached away long ago. Instead, not only has war between states been avoided for one hundred years, but the people of these states feel a relationship to one another and a responsibility for each other's well-being. Added to this is the safety of size, free trade, open communication and travel, and many other benefits citizens of tiny countries can never know until there is a world order based upon this model.

The pact does not face directly the arms race. The pact disarms all attempts to incite violent revolutions by offering to nations a peaceful means of social change, as well as increasingly strong incentives for peace and sanctions against violence. The problem of disarmament will become easier to solve as the pact grows in size, as citizens of all nations unite to insist on nonviolence, and as increased expansion and ease of trade between pact nations encourages would-be aggressors to consult and cooperate to preserve their economic interests.

A revolutionary, unmatched, and heretofore impossible factor is offering the global pact to the people of the world, instead of to the governments. Many of the people are uneducated, but they are highly intelligent and they love their children, as well as life itself. When they hear the offer of social change through peaceful means, and are told of the bloody and ruinous outcome of revolutions worldwide, the people of the world will begin, to whatever degree they are able, to promote the pact and encourage their leaders to join it. This is not forcing anything on the world; it is providing a choice. Great benefits will result when the people are as clearly aware and as firmly involved in the pact as are their leaders. There will be no chance of it being misused, nor will it suffer a lack of resources.

Concerning the success of the Pact, 'Abdu'l-Bahá says:

A few, unaware of the power latent in human endeavor, consider this matter as highly impracticable, nay even beyond the scope of man's utmost efforts. Such is not the case, however. . . . Endeavor, ceaseless endeavor, is required. Nothing short of an indomitable determination can possibly achieve it. Many a cause which past ages have regarded as purely visionary, yet in this day has become most easy and practicable. Why should this most great and lofty Cause . . . be regarded as impossible of achievement?[11]

Women: Champions of international peace. The most powerful force in recognizing the validity of the global pact in argument, securing its validity in law, and in propagating it—first nationally and then planetwide—is womankind. Women prominent in arenas of political life have had to contend with, and may have appeared to accept, the status quo. But, as they recognize the need for a new paradigm in human affairs, as they find they share sisterhood and motherhood across obsolete barriers of race, religion, nation, etc., as they realize that they—along with the men who have taken a stand for world peace and equity—constitute the vast majority of humankind, they will begin to move as a unit. 'Abdu'l-Bahá predicts:

She will refuse to give her sons for sacrifice upon the field of battle. In truth, she will be the greatest factor in establishing universal peace and international arbitration. Assuredly, woman will abolish warfare among mankind.[12]

. . . a real evidence of woman's superiority will be her service and efficiency in the establishment of universal peace.[13]

Women must make the greatest effort . . . until their enlightenment and striving succeeds in bringing about the unity of mankind.[14]

Women have traditionally depended on nonviolent methods to effect change. Women are not so psychologically dependent on the arms industry. They neither believe the nation, or any state within it, can survive economically only so long as wars endure, nor do they accept that the nation cannot tolerate the discomforts of the transition to a peacetime economy.[15] When there is suffering, women are accustomed to feeling the pain of others and taking direct action. They are not going to dismiss from their minds the possibility that life on earth could be destroyed. Many have lived their entire lives under threat of nuclear annihilation and seen their resources continually depleted by the cost of war; they will wait no longer for someone else to find the solution.

Women have been successfully testing their ability to bring about social change for half a century. They played the major part in establishing the principles listed above. They are a great part of the current peace movement. Creating dramatic positive change is a heady experience, vastly more invigorating than the tedious task of incorporating those changes into society and day-to-day life.

Women are ready for another great challenge. Their skills are honed, their various networks ready to connect, they are prepared physically, mentally, and spiritually and will move vigorously, joyously, fearlessly, unceasingly, and with powerful perseverance the moment the direction is clear.

World Religions: Working together for peace. The religions too, wield irresistable influence for the cause of freedom and peace. Unity of the religions does not mean they must all follow one creed; it means only that they must cooperate for their common benefit. Over the past few decades religions have become acquainted with each other. Many are discovering that they all worship one creative Power, by whatever name. At the least they are discovering they all require freedom if they are to follow their teachings, educate their children according to their beliefs, and propagate their faith and the culture that arises from that faith. They are discovering that they all have been assigned the responsibility to promote peace and relieve human suffering. There are already many instances wherein different faiths, or members of different faiths are working together to release their healing strength worldwide. Many of the peace groups are

Peace Groups and the Global Pact 93

within church congregations or are coalitions of religious communities.

When religions add their energy to that of the women of the world, and to that of those men and groups who have already taken a stand for freedom or peace, the impossible task will prove easy. All peoples and the majority of nations will surely sanction a global pact. The combined strength of the world's great faiths will be so mighty and widespread that opposition will be withdrawn. Trade, rather than arms, will necessarily become the main object of international consultation. It is already true that *". . . all the religious agencies will work for peace and promulgate the oneness of mankind."*[16]

This continent has a major role. America, too, has a vital role. American citizens are blood relatives to every people on earth: little wonder that we care about their suffering. We see their misery every day in our homes. We know other people long for freedom and security. We have the freedom, the resources, and the experienced ability to take individual and collective action wherever it is needed. 'Abdu'l-Bahá said:

> *The American people are indeed worthy of being the first to build the tabernacle of the great peace and proclaim the oneness of mankind. . . . This American nation is equipped and empowered to accomplish that which will adorn the pages of history . . . It will lead all nations spiritually.*[17]

The word "spiritual" does not mean the occult; spiritual attributes are godly qualities. 'Abdu'l-Bahá described this nation as influential, generous, idealistic, just, powerful, worthy, deserving, equipped, ready (to lead peace), reflective, noble, intelligent, progressive, secure, capable, spiritual, free. We must replace the paradigm of fear, anger, prejudice, isolationism, confrontation, and arms with that of confidence, communication, and creative, united action. This we can do.

It is not that we will force peace and freedom on the world. It is that we will begin to use every form of communication to remind all people that liberty and security are available if they want them and will make a persistent effort. United public affirmation is the means. All Americans who insist on peace with freedom for their children must lay aside differences of party, creed, race, wealth, etc., and must move as a unit. They must demand that their government take the first simple step of calling together a certain number of nations who are in accord to design the prototype and nucleus of the new world order.

All people of peace must arise. The role of the Bahá'ís in this, and of like-minded people everywhere, is to be the leaven which lifts the hearts, the hopes, the energy, the vision, and circle of influence, thereby empowering people of goodwill.[18] This is the first step, the most difficult to initiate and sustain. It demands that individuals strike a balance between hope for a better world and fear of annihilation, between world concerns and maintenance of the home, while courageously stepping out to lead, guide, and encourage.

Most of us have never lived without freedom. Few have seen the horrors of war firsthand. In our relative comfort and safety, we have avoided facing the reality of a world at risk. But finally the weapons of destruction are such that we can wait no longer. When the critical number of individuals have communicated the promise and details of the global pact to their friends, their groups, and their legislators, and their presidents, the concept will move on its own merit.

It appears that the task at hand is to build bridges; to understand the perspective and envision the objective of each individual and group we meet; to replace hopelessness, fear, estrangement, distrust, traditional competition, and conflict with assured, enthusiastic, united, public opinion. A call for peace with freedom must be raised that, in the words of 'Abdu'l-Bahá,

> ... *may exhilarate and rejoice the ears, ... bestow a new life, the different parties may become one party, the divergent ideas may disappear and revolve around one unique center, the East and the West of America may embrace each other, the anthem of the oneness of the world of humanity may confer a new life ..., and the Tabernacle of Universal Peace be pitched on the apex of America;—thus Europe and Africa may become vivified ..., this world may become another world ...* [19]

The Universal House of Justice, in its October 1985 statement to the peoples of the world, provided every nation, and the United Nations itself, the opportunity to initiate world order:

> With all the ardor of our hearts, we appeal to the leaders of all nations to seize this opportune moment and take irreversible steps to convoke this world meeting. All the forces of history impel the human race towards this act which will mark for all time the dawn of its long-awaited maturity. Will not the United Nations, with the full support of its membership, rise to the high purposes of such a crowning event? Let men and women, youth and children everywhere recognize the eternal merit of this imperative action for all peoples and lift up their voices in willing assent. Indeed, let it be this generation that inaugurates this glorious stage in the evolution of social life on the planet.[20]

It is up to each one of us to act. Until this matter is settled, no other problems can be solved. Because our resources are given to war, it is inevitable in fact that conditions will deteriorate. We must promulgate the global pact and raise the self-image, confidence, and joy of all people, thereby empowering them to action. The peace groups, already organized, motivated, and fearless, may be among our most important allies to carry the news of the pact to every segment of society.

This seemingly herculean undertaking may prove amazingly easy, for its time has come. So simple an action, formalizing existing bonds of national friendship and adding nations, one by one, whose people refuse to support war and insist upon Pact membership, will create a citadel of freedom so vast, strong, and far-reaching as to be unassailable.

Notes

This essay represents only the writer's individual understanding of the Bahá'í teachings discussed. Other Bahá'ís will hold views that differ.

    1. Shoghi Effendi, *Bahá'í Administration* (Wilmette, Ill.: Bahá'í Publishing Committee, 1928) p. 126. Shoghi Effendi, *Directives from the Guardian* (New Delhi: Bahá'í Publishing Trust, 1973) p. 83.

    2. Weigel, George, *Washington's Window on the World* (Seattle: Frayn Printing Co., 1982).

    3. Cf. 'Abdu'l-Bahá, *The Secret of Divine Civilization* (Wilmette, Ill.: Bahá'í Publishing Trust, 1957).

    4. Woito, Robert, *To End War* (New York: The Pilgrim Press, 1982).

    5. 'Abdu'l-Bahá, *The Foundations of World Unity*, (Wilmette, Ill.: Bahá'í Publishing Committee, 1945) p. 159.

    6. 'Abdu'l-Bahá, *Foundations of World Unity*, pp. 28–30.

    7. Shoghi Effendi, *World Order of Bahá'u'lláh* (Wilmette, Ill.: Bahá'í Publishing Committee, 1938) pp. 36–37.

    8. Esslemont, J. E., *Bahá'u'lláh and the New Era*, Rev. Ed. (Wilmette, Ill.: Bahá'í Publishing Trust, 1980) p. 166.

9. 'Abdu'l-Bahá, *Secret of Divine Civilization*, p. 64.
10. 'Abdu'l-Bahá, *Foundations of World Unity*, pp. 32–33.
11. Shoghi Effendi, *World Order of Bahá'u'lláh*, p. 38.
12. 'Abdu'l-Bahá, *The Promulgation of Universal Peace*, Rev. Ed. (Wilmette, Ill.: Bahá'í Publishing Trust, 1982) p. 108.
13. 'Abdu'l-Bahá, *Promulgation of Universal Peace*, p. 284.
14. 'Abdu'l-Bahá, *Paris Talks* (London: Bahá'í Publishing Trust, 1912) p. 163.
15. Anderson, Marion. *The Empty Porkbarrel* in *Defense Sense: The Search for a Rational Military Policy*.
16. 'Abdu'l-Bahá, *Secret of Divine Civilization*, p. 98.
17. 'Abdu'l-Bahá, *Promulgation of Universal Peace*, pp. 103–104.
18. Shoghi Effendi, *Citadel of Faith*, (Wilmette, Ill.: Bahá'í Publishing Trust, 1965) p. 127.
19. 'Abdu'l-Bahá, *Tablets of the Divine Plan* (Wilmette, Ill.: Bahá'í Publishing Trust, 1959) p. 47.
20. Universal House of Justice, *The Promise of World Peace*, Statement to the Peoples of the World, October 1985.

Bringing In The Dawn: Women and Peace

by Susan Brill

IN AN INTERESTING AND CHALLENGING ESSAY, "The Future—If There Is One—Is Female," Sally Miller Gearhart points out that in order to achieve a peaceful and nonviolent world, we must all, women and men, affirm in ourselves those "characteristics historically associated with the female; specifically: empathy, nurturance and cooperation."[1] Sandra Harding, a professor of philosophy at the University of Delaware, discussed the divergent views of rationality (i.e., expressions of rational belief and action) held by women and men, in her paper "Is Gender a Variable in Conceptions of Rationality? A Survey of Issues." She explains that "a rational person, for women, values highly her abilities to empathize and 'connect' with particular others and wants to learn more complex and satisfying ways to take the role of the particular other in relationships. . . . For men, in contrast, a rational person values highly his ability to separate himself from others and to make decisions independent of what others think—to develop 'autonomy.' "[2]

It is through this very process of objectification, distancing ourselves from other people, other creatures, other nations, other climes, that we are able to perceive of others and act toward them in ways that would be abhorrent if turned on ourselves. By means of developing our capacities of nurturance, empathy, intuition, love, and service will a major step be taken toward ending the violence rampant in our world today and bringing forth a more united and peaceful world. 'Abdu'l-Bahá pointed out in 1911 that *"the balance is already shifting . . . the spiritual qualities . . . in which woman is strong, are gaining ascendancy. Hence the new age will be an age less masculine and more permeated with the feminine ideals."*[3]

This paper will explore the question of women and world peace, and how they are interrelated from one Bahá'í's perspective. These concepts will then be explored in terms of contemporary feminist thought and theory, with a detailed look at the current state of our world as it relates to peace (or the lack thereof) and women.

As 'Abdu'l-Bahá mentioned, *"the balance is already shifting."* The world, and its needs, are changing. As Arthur O'Shaughnessy put it in his wonderful poem "Ode":

> For each age is a dream that is dying,
> Or one that is coming to birth.[4]

'Abdu'l-Bahá said in Paris that *"religion should unite all hearts and cause wars and disputes to vanish from the face of the earth; it should give birth to spirituality, and bring light and life to every soul. If religion becomes a cause of dislike, hatred and division it would be better to be without it, and to withdraw from such a religion would be a truly religious act."*[5] From the Bahá'í perspective, the very purpose of religion is the unification of humankind.

In *The World Order of Bahá'u'lláh*, Shoghi Effendi, the Guardian of the Bahá'í Faith, wrote:

> Unity of family, of tribe, of city-state, and nation have been successively attempted and fully established. World unity is the goal towards which a harassed humanity is

striving. Nation-building has come to an end. The anarchy inherent in state sovereignty is moving towards a climax. A world, growing to maturity, must abandon this fetish, recognize the oneness and wholeness of human relationships, and establish once for all the machinery that can best incarnate this fundamental principle of its life.[6]

Bahá'u'lláh wrote in the Tablet of the World that *"it is not his to boast who loveth his country, but it is his who loveth the world."*[7] And again in the Tablet to the Leaders is written: *"Today, this Servant has assuredly come to vivify the world and to bring into unity all who are on the face of the earth. That which God willeth shall come to pass and thou shalt see the earth even as the Abhá (Most Glorious) Paradise."*[8]

The Bahá'í Writings are very clear about the importance of world peace, and even more specifically about the role that women will play therein. 'Abdu'l-Bahá stated that *"in truth, she will be the greatest factor in establishing universal peace and international arbitration. Assuredly, women will abolish warfare among mankind."*[9] Women, as the mothers of the world, will refuse to sacrifice their children to war. *"When perfect equality shall be established between men and women, peace may be realized for the simple reason that womankind in general will never favor warfare. Women will not be willing to allow those whom they have so tenderly cared for to go to the battlefield. When they shall have a vote, they will oppose any cause of warfare."*[10] The importance of universal suffrage was strongly emphasized by 'Abdu'l-Bahá, so much so that he connected this issue directly to that of international peace. *"The most momentous question of this day is international peace and arbitration, and universal peace is impossible without universal suffrage."*[11]

A number of the early Bahá'í women in the West, like Laura Dreyfus-Barney and Martha Root, were active in the women's suffrage movement, but the achievement of universal suffrage will not be sufficient to bring about world peace.

'Abdu'l-Bahá explained that women must become active participants in world affairs, for women will neither *"sanction war, nor be satisfied with it. So it will come to pass that when women participate fully and equally in the affairs of the world, when they enter confidently and capably the great arena of laws and politics, war will cease; for woman will be the obstacle and hindrance to it. This is true and without doubt."*[12]

Clearly woman has a great part to play in the advent of world peace. An understanding of the Bahá'í teachings on the equality of the sexes and on the nature of woman will clarify why it is woman, and not man, who will bring peace to the world. In a talk delivered in Paris on November 14, 1912, 'Abdu'l-Bahá discussed these issues:

> *In the world of humanity we find a great difference* [between the sexes]; *the female sex is treated as though inferior, and is not allowed equal rights and privileges. This condition is due not to nature, but to education. In the Divine Creation there is no such distinction. Neither sex is superior to the other in the sight of God. . . . If women received the same educational advantages as those of men, the result would demonstrate the equality of capacity of both for scholarship. . . . Women must endeavour then to attain greater perfection, to be man's equal in every respect, to make progress in all in which she has been backward, so that man will be compelled to acknowledge her equality of capacity and attainment. . . . When men own the equality of women there will be no need for them to struggle for their rights! One of the principles then of Bahá'u'lláh is the equality of sex.*[13]

Woman is the equal of man. As one Bahá'í put it, "For the first time in religious history, equality of the sexes stands as an inherent spiritual principle, part of the Word of God."[14] Yet 'Abdu'l-Bahá has further explained that *"in some respects woman is superior to man. She is more tender-hearted, more receptive, her intuition is more intense. . . . In the necessity of life, woman is more instinct with power than man, for to her he owes his very existence.*"¹⁵ And again in addressing womankind, he wrote, "*Blessed are ye! Blessed are ye! Verily ye are worthy of every gift. Verily ye deserve to adorn your heads with the crown of everlasting glory, because in sciences and arts, in virtues and perfections ye shall become equal to man, and as regards tenderness of heart and the abundance of mercy and sympathy ye are superior.*"¹⁶

It is these areas in which woman is innately superior to man that will propel her to bring about greater peace in the world. This was explained by 'Abdu'l-Bahá while aboard the S.S. Cedric, upon its arrival in New York in 1911:

*The world in the past has been ruled by force, and man has dominated over woman by reason of his more forceful and aggressive qualities both of body and mind. But the balance is already shifting; force is losing its dominance, and mental alertness, intuition, and the spiritual qualities of love and service, in which woman is strong, are gaining ascendancy. Hence the new age will be an age less masculine and more permeated with the feminine ideals, or, to speak more exactly, will be an age in which the masculine and feminine elements of civilization will be more evenly balanced.*¹⁷

The challenge and responsibility of ushering in universal peace rests upon the shoulders of womankind. To woman 'Abdu'l-Bahá gave this charge:

Therefore, strive to show in the human world that women are most capable and efficient, that their hearts are more tender and susceptible than the hearts of men, that they are more philanthropic and responsive toward the needy and suffering, that they are inflexibly opposed to war and are lovers of peace. Strive that the ideal of international peace may become realized through the efforts of womankind, for man is more inclined to war than woman, and a real evidence of woman's superiority will be her service and efficiency in the establishment of universal peace.[18]

From this Bahá'í perspective, it is seen that woman's role in the establishment of peace throughout the world will be very great. But just what is meant by this is not clear without an understanding of universal peace. The definitions of these terms (as supplied by various dictionaries) are most illuminating. *Peace* is qualified most often in the Bahá'í Writings by the adjective *universal,* which carries with it a variety of significations: 1) present or occurring throughout the whole world; 2) existent everywhere or under all conditions; 3) pertinent to all of humankind; 4) of or belonging to all nature; 5) constituting or forming, existing or regarded as, a complete whole. The term *peace* is defined as follows: 1) a state of quiet or tranquillity; 2) freedom from civil disturbance; 3) absence of war, mutual concord between governments; 4) a state of security within a community; 5) freedom from violence; 6) a mental or spiritual condition marked by freedom from disquieting or oppressive thoughts or emotions; 7) freedom from outside disturbance or harassment; 8) harmony in human or personal relations.[19]

The above stated definitions of the terms *universal* and *peace* indicate that what Bahá'ís should understand by *universal peace* is something much broader than simply freedom from world war or nuclear annihilation. The peace that women are to usher in is a peace that is global, touches all nations, all of humankind, and all of nature. And this peace is one that assures nations, communities, homes and families, and individuals of their freedom from discord, oppression, violence, harassment, and insecurity. Jo Vellacott put this idea of peace quite clearly in a 1981 lecture sponsored by the Friends General Conference: "Whether we speak of peace on a personal level, a family level, within our organizations, nationally or internationally, we must recognize that true peace exists only where all can be reasonably free of fear, and have opportunity for the exercise of body, mind, and spirit."[20]

The breadth and depth of the concept of universal peace truly incorporates the theory behind the feminist slogan that "the personal is political," for universal peace touches individuals as well as governments. Sixty years ago in a talk to the Los Angeles City Club, Laura Dreyfus-Barney, an early Bahá'í and a peace advocate, drew the connection between individuals' behaviors and those of nations:

> We must make the youth of the world realize that the moral code of the individual must be applied to the relations between nations. Theft, attack, rapine, all the crimes for which the laws of a nation penalize the individual, must be handled in an identical manner by a court or arbitration world court, league of nations or what you will.
>
> Once we have made the youth of the world realize this fundamental premise, we shall have taken the first tremendous step to end war and all its miseries.[21]

Not only must war be ended to bring about universal peace, but so must there be an end to rape, battery, child molestation, the pollution of our natural resources, marketing of dangerous and unhealthy products (e.g., "foods" with little, if any, nutritional value, but riddled with preservatives and assorted, sordid chemicals). Donna Warnock, a peace activist, explained in her paper, "Patriarchy Is a Killer: What People Concerned About Peace and Justice Should Know," that "the mentality that builds nuclear weapons is the same one that rapes women and destroys the natural environment."[22] This very connection, that "the personal is political," is made very poignantly in a powerful poem by June Jordan (poet, activist, feminist, professor). This poem is entitled *Poem about My Rights:*

Even tonight and I need to take a walk and clear
my head about this poem about why I can't
go out without changing my clothes my shoes
my body posture my gender identity my age
my status as a woman alone in the evening/
alone on the streets/ alone not being the point/
the point being that I can't do what I want
to do with my own body because I am the wrong
sex the wrong age the wrong skin and
suppose it was not here in the city but down on the
   beach/
or far into the woods and I wanted to go
there by myself thinking about God/ or thinking
about children or thinking about the world/ all of it
disclosed by the stars and the silence:
I could not go and I could not think and I could not
stay there
alone
as I need to be
alone because I can't do what I want to do with my own
body . . .
I am very familiar with the problems of the C.I.A.
and the problems of South Africa and the problems
of Exxon Corporation and the problems of white
America in general and the problems of the teachers
and the preachers and the F.B.I. and the social
workers and my particular Mom and Dad/ I am very
familiar with the problems because the problems
turn out to be
me
I am the history of rape
I am the history of the rejection of who I am
I am the history of the terrorized incarceration of
my self
I am the history of battery assault and limitless
armies against whatever I want to do with my mind

and my body and my soul and
whether it's about walking out at night
or whether it's about the love that I feel or
whether it's about the sanctity of my vagina or
the sanctity of my national boundaries
or the sanctity of my leaders or the sanctity
of each and every desire
that I know from my personal and idiosyncratic
and indisputably single and singular heart
I have been raped
be-
cause I have been wrong the wrong sex the wrong age
the wrong skin the wrong nose the wrong hair the
wrong need the wrong dream the wrong geographic
the wrong sartorial I
I have been the meaning of rape . . .
but let this be unmistakable this poem
is not consent I do not consent
to my mother to my father to the teachers to
the F.B.I. to South Africa to Bedford-Stuy
to Park Avenue to American Airlines to the hardon
idlers on the corners to the sneaky creeps in
cars
I am not wrong: Wrong is not my name
My name is my own my own my own
and I can't tell you who the hell set things up like this
but I can tell you that from now on my resistance
my simple and daily and nightly self-determination
may very well cost you your life[23]

This poem deals with a lot of different issues from rape, assault and battery, to the C.I.A. and the F.B.I. and South Africa. But what is critical to the poem is the connection Jordan draws between seemingly different concerns. It is the same oppressive patriarchal mentality that leads to racism, sexism, nationalism, battery, hegemony, and rape.

Beyond these concepts, however, is the anger that is heard in Jordan's poem. This anger comes out strongly in parts of the poem by her use of repetition throughout the poem:

> ... I can't
> go out without changing my clothes my shoes
> my body posture my gender identity my age
> my status as a woman alone in the evening/
> alone on the streets ...

And again:

> ... I have been wrong the wrong sex the wrong age
> the wrong skin the wrong nose the wrong hair the
> wrong need the wrong dream the wrong geographic
> the wrong sartorial I ...

And finally "My name is my own my own my own."

June Jordan is angry and she wants her anger heard and she wants to be understood. And to underscore her anger at the way things are and her urgent desire for change, she ends the poem with her own personal threat.

June Jordan is angry. Women are angry. Blacks are angry. Hispanics are angry. Native Americans are angry. The poor are angry. Gay men and lesbians are angry. Vietnam veterans are angry. The disabled are angry. And Alice Walker, the author of *The Color Purple*, is angry.

She delivered a speech three years ago at an antinuclear rally in San Francisco. Her speech, excerpted here, is a powerful statement from a black woman, like Jordan, who must deal with the double oppressions of racism and sexism.

> When I have considered the enormity of the white man's crimes against humanity. Against women. Against every living person of color. Against the poor. Against my

mother and my father. Against me. . . . When I consider that he is, they are, a real and present threat to my life and the life of my daughter, my people, I think: Let the earth marinate in poisons. Let the bombs cover the ground like rain. For nothing short of total destruction will ever teach them anything.

And it would be good, perhaps, to put an end to the species in any case, rather than let white men continue to subjugate it, and continue their lust to dominate, exploit and despoil not just our planet, but the rest of the universe—which is their clear and oftstated intention, leaving their arrogance and litter not just on the moon, but on everything else they can reach.

If we have any true love for the stars, planets, the rest of Creation, we must do everything we can to keep white men away from them. They who have appointed themselves our representatives to the rest of the universe. They who have never met any new creature without exploiting, abusing or destroying it. They who say we poor and colored and female and elderly blight neighborhoods, while they blight worlds.

Under the white man every star would become a South Africa, every planet a Vietnam.

Fatally eradicating ourselves may in fact be the only way to save others from what Earth has already become. And this is a consideration that I believe requires serious thought from every one of us."[24]

Alice Walker is an angry woman. I, too, am an angry woman; but unlike Alice Walker, I, as a Bahá'í, do not believe that total annihilation is necessary. And unlike June Jordan, I do not advocate violent actions, but rather nonviolent ones. Our anger is important. We all must be aware of the horrific situation of our world today. As 'Abdu'l-Bahá has written:

..nnot be shown the tyrant, the deceiver, or the
...use, far from awakening them to the error of their
...naketh them to continue in their perversity as before.
...ter how much kindliness ye may expend upon the liar,
he w..l but lie the more, for he believeth you to be deceived,
while ye understand him but too well, and only remain silent
out of your extreme compassion.[25]

And elsewhere 'Abdu'l-Bahá has explained that if we *"exercise [our] anger and wrath against the bloodthirsty tyrants who are like ferocious beasts, it is very praiseworthy."*[26]

It is this anger that makes us work for change, that empowers us as we refuse to be oppressed any longer, and that leads us to educate our oppressors to change themselves.

The anger heard in *Poem about My Rights* can be defined as an affliction. Barbara Deming, a civil rights activist, pacifist, lesbian, discussed this type of anger in a paper delivered at the 1971 War Resisters' League national conference. She says that one type of anger is not helpful and can be described as an affliction:

> This anger asserts to another not: "You must change and you can change"—but: "Your very existence is a threat to my very existence." It speaks not hope but fear. The fear is: you can't change—and I can't change if you are still there. It asserts not: change! but: drop dead! . . .
> Our task of course, is to transmute the anger that is affliction into the anger that is determination to bring about change. I think, in fact, that one could give that as a definition of revolution."[27]

Revolution is truly what is needed, and is what will come. The world is revolving, and the future will be an age, according to 'Abdu'l-Bahá, *"more permeated with the feminine ideals."* Many female writers have affirmed this in essays, novels, and poetry. Barbara Zanotti, in her essay, "Patriarchy: A State of War," writes that "women are the bearers of lifeloving energy. Ours is the task of deepening that passion for life and separating from all that threatens life, all that diminishes life; becoming who we are as women; telling/living the truth of our lives; shifting the weight of the world."[28]

This very idea of change is looked at in relation to rape by Pat James, a self-defense instructor and coordinator of the Women's School in Philadelphia. "It is women who will end rape—by rejecting stereotypes and embracing life-affirming self-images; by depending upon ourselves and each other for protection; by changing the conditions of our lives, and by working to change the conditions in men's lives that nourish a rapist culture."[29]

This is the very process of empowerment, our realizing our own power and capabilities and moving from a state of psychological disability to one of enabling personal power. And only through this process of personal empowerment can we as individuals rise up to demand, and work for, those changes so desperately needed in the world today. Jane Meyerding, radical feminist and pacifist, in her article "Reclaiming Nonviolence," comments that "the empowerment of previously disempowered individuals thus has a ripple effect on society, because the norm for empowered individuals or groups becomes change rather than stasis. . . . In contrast to violent methods of social change which tend to concentrate and centralize power, the newly realized power activated by nonviolent empowerment is 'personalized'—autonomous and decentralized."[30]

In a letter that 'Abdu'l-Bahá himself has described as a "very important tablet," he speaks of his feelings in relation to the horrors of war:

My spirit is aflame and burning; my heart is broken, mournful, heavy and despondent; my eyes are weeping and my soul is on fire. Oh! I am so bowed down and sorrowful.

And addressing the Bahá'ís he continues:

> *O people! Weep and cry, lament and bemoan your fate. Then hasten ye, perchance ye may become able to extinguish with the water of newborn ideals of spiritual democracy and celestial freedom, this many-flamed, world-consuming fire, and through your heaven-inspired resolution you may usher in the Golden Era of International Solidarity and World Confederation.*[31]

Individual empowerment is the basis of the Bahá'í Faith and one of the reasons why there is no need for clergy within the religion. Bahá'u'lláh has written:

> *Arise, O people, and by the power of God's might, resolve to gain the victory over your own selves, that haply the whole earth may be freed and sanctified from its servitude to the gods of its idle fancies—gods that have inflicted such loss upon, and are responsible for the misery of, their wretched worshippers. These idols form the obstacle that impeded man in his efforts to advance in the path of perfection.*

For Bahá'ís and many others, the source of our power comes from our being in touch with our spirituality. *"The source of courage and power is the promotion of the Word of God, and steadfastness in His Love."*[32]

Jo Vellacott, a Quaker, writes, "The people whom I know who live a truly nonviolent life are in touch with the source of power, call it what you will: the Light, the seed, God, the holy spirit."[33] And by plugging ourselves into the source of our powers, and by being enabled anew, we can begin "to labor serenely, confidently, and unremittingly to lend our share of assistance, in whichever way circumstances may enable us, to the operation of the forces which, as marshalled and directed by Bahá'u'lláh, are leading humanity out of the valley of misery and shame."[34] 'Abdu'l-Bahá has explained that the standards and powers of the past are not sufficient for the present.

> *That which was applicable to human needs during the early history of the race can neither meet nor satisfy the demands of this day, this period of newness and consummation. Humanity has emerged from its former state of limitation and preliminary training. Man must now become imbued with new virtues and powers, new moral standards, new capacities.*[35]

The idea of new virtues, new standards, new capacities is brought out in a poem by Joan Cavanagh. In her poem, entitled "I Am a Dangerous Woman," the very concept of danger takes on new meaning: woman is dangerous—not to the world, but rather to the powers that be—because she offers, and insists on, change from men's ways of violence and destruction to a world of nurturance, motherhood, life.

> I am a dangerous woman
> Carrying neither bombs nor babies
> Flowers nor molotov cocktails.
> I confound all your reason, theory, realism
> Because I will neither lie in your ditches
> Nor dig your ditches for you
> Nor join in your armed struggle
> For bigger and better ditches.
> I will not walk with you nor walk for you,
> I won't live with you
> And I won't die for you,
> But neither will I try to deny you
> Your right to live and die.
> I will not share one square foot of this earth with you
> While you're hell-bent on destruction,
> But neither will I deny that we are of the same earth,
> Born of the same Mother.

> I will not permit
> You to bind my life to yours
> But I will tell you that our lives
> Are bound together
> And I will demand
> That you live as though you understand
> This one salient fact.[36]

This poem is essentially a poem of love for the life of our planet, our children, our women, and our men. It is a song of the past, a description of our present. But even more importantly, it is a song and cry for the future. For Cavanagh, it is from our knowledge of our world and our love for humanity and Mother Earth, that we will be "dangerous"—a threat to the status quo, a source of change, empowered to serve humankind positively.

Daniel C. Jordan, a Bahá'í educator, explained in his article "Becoming Your True Self," that "the development of one's knowing and loving capacities in service to mankind" is the very process of "becoming one's true self."[37] And this is what is intended herein by empowerment—our becoming our true selves, becoming enabled. Jordan further explained that, for Bahá'ís, the development of our knowing and loving capacities in relation to God is the animating, or empowering, purpose behind our creation. If to be empowered by our knowledge of, and love for, our world is to be a danger, a threat to the world as we know it today, then we all must become "dangerous" women and men.

Cavanagh is an angry woman. She is angry about the state our world is in. Her anger is that which empowers and leads to change. Audre Lorde, in the keynote presentation at the National Women's Studies Association Conference in 1981, pointed out that "anger is loaded with information and energy."[38] If to look at our world makes us angry, then this is a good thing; for it is through our anger that our struggles will intensify and be heightened.

What is the information/knowledge/wisdom that angers

women today? What is the source of our fury? A look at our world is enlightening:

☐ Women are approximately 52% of the world's population, grow 50% of the world's food, head 30% of the world's households. Meanwhile, they earn 10% of the world's income and own 1% of the world's property.[39]

☐ In 1969, 35% of poverty level families in the United States were headed by women, and 51% of minority families were headed by women. By 1979, 50% of poverty level families were maintained by women, and 75% of black families were. American women, on the average, earn 60% of what men earn.[40]

☐ Half of the 8.4 million single elderly women receiving Social Security benefits in the U.S. live at or near the poverty line. In 1983, the median annual income for all women over age sixty-five from all sources was $5,599, compared to $9,766 for men. Disabled women workers receive an average monthly benefit of $371, compared to $519 for disabled men.[41]

☐ Of women in prison in the United States, 70% were first arrested for prostitution. 80% of juveniles who become prostitutes were victims of incest in their own families.[42]

☐ In 85% of American domestic homicide cases, the police had been called for help previously by the battered wives.[43]

☐ According to a 1968 study, 35% of Puerto Rican women of childbearing age had been sterilized, primarily through government financed programs.[44] 25% of all Native American women have been sterilized.[45]

☐ An intrauterine device (IUD), the Dalkon Shield, was placed by doctors in about 4 million women in the early 1970s. Almost immediately it began producing dangerous side effects. Over 1 million have suffered acute pelvic infections, 1 in 5 are sterile, and a number have died.[46]

☐ 60% of mind-altering drugs are prescribed for women,

as are 71% of antidepressants, and 80% of amphetamines.[47]

☐ Of the 690,000 hysterectomies performed in the United States in 1979, only 1 in 5 could be justified as clinically necessary on the basis of life-threatening medical needs.[48]

☐ In Guinea, 85% of all women are excised.[49] (Excision is the removal of the clitoris and adjacent parts of the labia minora, or all of the genitalia except the labia majora.)

☐ Clitoridectomy (removal of the clitoris) is still commonly performed in over thirty countries in Africa, Arabia, and the Middle East.[50]

☐ Infibulation (excision, followed by the sewing up of the genitals to close the entrance to the vagina, except for a tiny opening required for urination) is also widespread. The opening is finally cut open before a woman's wedding night.[51]

☐ There are about 180,000 illegal abortions performed each year in Portugal. About 2,000 women die each year as a result of these operations.[52]

☐ In Italy, approximately 3 million illegal abortions are performed each year.[53]

☐ In the United States, more than 1½ million women choose abortion.[54]

☐ In the United States, every 5 minutes a woman is raped, and rape is the most frequently committed and fastest growing crime in America.[55] Every 3 minutes a woman is beaten by her male partner.[56] 50–70% of wives experience battery during their marriages.[57] Every 10 minutes a little girl is molested.[58] About 1½ million children under the age of sixteen are used annually in commerical sex, including prostitution and pornography.[59]

In light of all these facts, it is certainly not surprising that women around the world are angry. Having felt the brunt of the patriarchy's oppression for unnumbered centuries, women acutely feel the need for change. As mothers of the world, we are especially concerned for the future—for our children's sakes, and for their children's.

Cavanagh correctly said in her poem, "Masculinity has made this world a living hell."[60] Gearhart reiterates 'Abdu'l-Bahá's statement when she asserts that "Either the future is female or the future is not."[61] We, as women, are realizing this: we are being empowered by our anger at what men have done to our world and by our hopes and visions for the future. Throughout the world women have been, and are, continuing to be active in working for a nonviolent world.

A part of Ellen Bass's poem "Our Stunning Harvest" reads:

> Women, I want
> to gather with you.
> Our numbers are grand.
> Our hands are capable, practiced,
> our minds know pattern, know
> relationship, how the tree
> pulls water up through root
> through trunk, through branch, stem
> into leaf, how the surface stomata release
> water vapor into the air, the air cooled. We know
> to honor trees. We know
> the chrysalis, the grub, the earthworm.
>
> We have handled baby poop and vomit
> the incontinence of the old and sick.
> We smell menses every month
> from the time we are young girls.
> We do not faint.
> We do not titter
> at mice.
> We have handled money
> and the lack of it
> and we have survived

poverty, puerperal fever
forceps, scopolamine
footbinding, excision, infibulation
beatings, thorazine, diet pills
rape, witch burning, valium, chin lifts
female infanticide, child molestation
breast x-rays, suttee.

Some of us have died. Millions, millions
have been killed, murdered. We
mourn, we mourn
their courage, their innocence
their wisdom often lost to us.
We remember.
We are fierce
like a cornered animal.
Our fury spurts like geysers
like volcanoes, brilliant lava, molten gold
cascading in opulent plumes.

And every morning we gather eggs from the chickens
we milk the goat
or drive to the Safeway and push our cart
under fluorescent lights.
We feed our children.

We feed them blood from our womb
milk at our breast.
Our bodies create and nourish life.

We can gather.
We can save our earth.
We can labor like we labored
to birth our babies,
laboring past thirst, past the rising and the setting of
  the sun
    past distraction, past demands
past the need to pee, to cry, or even to live

into the consuming pain
    pain
pain beyond possibility,
until there is nothing but the
inevitable gathering
gathering, gathering
and
the new is born,
relief spreading through us
like the wave after cresting
spreads over sand in a shush of foam, grace
our saving grace. . . .

NO touch bee
BITE my finger
my daughter explains to me
pulling back her hand from the wild radish blossoms
    buzzing with furry bees.

My child
with your neck still creased in slight folds
the tiny white hairs of your back stemming up your spine
fanning out over shoulders like a fern,
you *may* live
you *may*, you *may*, oh I want to believe it is possible
that you may live
to handle bees, pick miner's lettuce
eat black olives in the sun,
  to gather,
    with me
      with your daughters
        with all the world's life-sweet women,
          our stunning harvest.[62]

Let us work toward our stunning harvest. But in order to do so, we must be aware of where we are now. As Barbara Deming learned, to run "away from the truths of [our] own experience is not only useless but also self-defeating and disempowering."[63] And through our knowledge and love and anger will we become empowered to work for change—in ourselves and in our world. Our charge is to speak by our actions "in ways that open the minds of others to radical insights about our present condition, and to the courage to trust this new vision and to act upon it themselves."[64]

As Marilyn French wrote in her new book, *Beyond Power: On Women, Men, and Morals*, "We all have power—the capacity to influence, alter, affect the lives of those around us. And until all of us use our power in the public world, it will continue to be dominated by those who are driven to domination, rather than by those who wish to use power as a means to noncontrolling well-being."[65] Let me repeat Bahá'u'lláh's exhortation to us: "*Arise, O people, and by the power of God's might, resolve to gain the victory over your own selves, that haply the whole earth may be freed and sanctified from its servitude to the gods of its idle fancies—gods that have inflicted such loss upon, and are responsible for the misery of, their wretched worshipers.*"[66]

Let me end with the words of Marilyn French. "The goal—feminizing the world—is also the means—feminizing our worlds. The end is the process: integrating ourselves and carrying integration as far into the world as we can. There is no final end; there is only the doing well, being what we want to be, doing what we want to do, living in delight. The choice lies between a life lived through and a life lived; between . . . fragmentation and integration. The choice may be between death and life."[67]

Let us work together for universal peace, with complete awareness of the immensity of the task before us. Let us work together for a nonviolent world in which all peoples, women and men, black, Hispanic, Native American, and white, poor and rich, old and young, religious and nonreligious, gay and straight, disabled, fat or thin, can live together in peace and harmony. Let us set free the oppressors amongst us, as well as the oppressed.

Let us bring in the dawn.[68]

Notes

1. Sally Miller Gearhart, "The Future—If There Is One—Is Female," *Reweaving the Web of Life: Feminism and Nonviolence* (Philadelphia: New Society Press, 1982) p. 271.
2. Sandra Harding, "Is Gender a Variable in Conceptions of Reality? A Survey of Issues," *Beyond Domination* (U.S.A.: Rowmon & Allanheld, Pub., 1983) pp. 52–3.
3. 'Abdu'l-Bahá, quoted in John Esslemont, *Bahá'u'lláh and the New Era* (Wilmette, Ill.: Bahá'í Publishing Trust, 1980) p. 149.
4. Arthur O'Shaughessy, *Poems of Arthur O'Shaughessy*, edited by W. A. Percy (Westport, Conn.: Greenwood Press, 1979) p. 39.
5. 'Abdu'l-Bahá, quoted in *Bahá'u'lláh and the New Era*, p. 158.
6. Shoghi Effendi, *The World Order of Bahá'u'lláh* (Wilmette, Ill.: Bahá'í Publishing Trust, 1938) p. 202.
7. Bahá'u'lláh, quoted in *Bahá'u'lláh and the New Era*, p. 161.
8. Ibid., p. 156.
9. 'Abdu'l-Bahá, *The Promulgation of Universal Peace* (Wilmette, Ill.: Bahá'í Publishing Trust, 1982) p. 108.
10. Ibid., p. 167.
11. Ibid., p. 134.
12. Ibid., p. 135.
13. 'Abdu'l-Bahá, *Paris Talks* (London: Bahá'í Publishing Trust, 1912 [1971]) pp. 161–3.
14. Ann Schoonmaker, "Revisioning the Woman's Movement," in *Circle of Unity: Bahá'í Approaches to Current Social Issues* (Los Angeles: Kalimát Press, 1984) p. 145.
15. 'Abdu'l-Bahá, *Paris Talks*, pp. 161–2.
16. Ibid., p. 184.
17. 'Abdu'l-Bahá, quoted in *Bahá'u'lláh and the New Era*, p. 149.
18. 'Abdu'l-Bahá, *The Promulgation of Universal Peace*, p. 284.

19. *Webster's Third New International Dictionary* (unabridged), (Springfield, Mass.: G & C Merriam Co., 1981); *The Oxford English Dictionary* (Oxford: Clarendon Press, 1978); *Funk & Wagnalls Standard Dictionary* (New York: Funk & Wagnalls Co.).

20. Jo Vellacott, "Women, Peace & Power," *Reweaving the Web of Life: Feminism and Nonviolence*, p. 37.

21. Laura Dreyfus-Barney, quoted in Karla Jay, "The Amazon Was a Pacifist," *Reweaving the Web of Life: Feminism and Nonviolence*, p. 104.

22. Donna Warnock, "Patriarchy Is a Killer: What People Concerned About Peace and Justice Should Know," *Reweaving the Web of Life: Feminism and Nonviolence*, pp. 27–8.

23. June Jordan, "Poem about My Rights," *passion* (Boston: Beacon Press, 1980) pp. 86–9.

24. Alice Walker, "Only Justice Can Stop A Curse," *Reweaving the Web of Life: Feminism and Nonviolence*, op. cit., pp. 264–5.

25. 'Abdu'l-Bahá, *Selections from the Writings of 'Abdu'l-Bahá* (Haifa: Bahá'í World Center, 1978) p. 158.

26. 'Abdu'l-Bahá, *Bahá'í World Faith* (Wilmette, Ill.: Bahá'í Publishing Trust, 1943) p. 320.

27. Barbara Deming, "On Anger," *We Are All Part of One Another* (Philadelphia: New Society Publishers, 1984) p. 213.

28. Barbara Zanotti, "Patriarchy: A State of War," *Reweaving the Web of Life: Feminism and Nonviolence*, p. 19.

29. Pat James, "Physical Resistance to Attack: The Pacifist's Dilemma, The Feminist's Hope," ibid., p. 390.

30. Jane Meyerding, "Reclaiming Nonviolence: some thoughts for feminist womyn who used to be nonviolent, and vice versa," ibid., pp. 10–11.

31. 'Abdu'l-Bahá, quoted in *Star of the West*, vol. 5, no. 16.

32. Bahá'u'lláh, *Bahá'í World Faith* (Wilmette, Illinois: Bahá'í Publishing Trust, 1943 [1976]), pp. 139 and 141.

33. Jo Vellacott, "Women, Peace & Power," p. 34.

34. Shoghi Effendi, *The Promised Day is Come* (Wilmette, Ill.: Bahá'í Publishing Trust, 1941 [1980]) p. 124.

35. 'Abdu'l-Bahá, quoted in *The Promised Day is Come*, p. 119.

36. Joan Cavanagh, "I Am a Dangerous Woman," *Reweaving the Web of Life: Feminism and Nonviolence*, pp. 3–4.

37. Daniel C. Jordan, "Becoming Your True Self," *World Order*, vol. 3, no. 1, (Fall 1968).

38. Audre Lorde, "The Uses of Anger: Women Responding to Racism," *Sister Outsider* (Trumansburg, New York: The Crossing Press, 1984) p. 127.
39. "A Shift in the Wind," *The Hunger Project Newspaper*, no. 21 (April, 1985) p. 7.
40. *20 Facts on Women Workers* (Washington, D.C.: U.S. Department of Labor—Women's Bureau, 1980) pp. 1-3.
41. "Social Security Is a Woman's Issue," *National NOW Times*, vol. XVIII, no. 3 (Washington, D.C.: The National Organization for Women) p. 10.
42. *Crimes Against Women: Proceedings of the International Tribunal*, ed. by Diana E. H. Russell and Nicole Vande Ven (East Palo Alto, Calif.: Frog in the Well, 1984) p. 180.
43. Ibid., p. 145.
44. Ibid., p. 27.
45. Donna Warnock, "Patriarchy," p. 25.
46. Robert S. Mendelsohn, M.D., *Male Practice: How Doctors Manipulate Women* (Chicago: Contemporary Books, Inc., 1981) p. 35.
47. Ibid., p. 60.
48. Ibid., p. 97.
49. *Crimes Against Women*, pp. 151-2.
50. Mary Daly, *Gyn/ecology: The Metaethics of Radical Feminism* (Boston: Beacon Press, 1978) p. 161.
51. Ibid., p. 167.
52. *Crimes Against Women*, p. 9.
53. Ibid., p. 22.
54. Ellen Goodman, "Forgotten in abortion debate," *The Boston Globe* (January 31, 1985) p. 15.
55. Donna Warnock, "Patriarchy," p. 20.
56. Ibid.
57. Robin Morgan, ed., *Sisterhood Is Global* (Garden City, New York: Anchor Books, 1984) p. 703.
58. Donna Warnock, "Patriarchy," p. 20.
59. Ibid., p. 419.
60. Joan Cavanagh, "I Am a Dangerous Woman," *Reweaving the Web of Life: Feminism and Nonviolence*, pp. 3-4.
61. Sally Miller Gearhart, "The Future—If There Is One—Is Female," *Reweaving the Web of Life: Feminism and Nonviolence*, p. 284.

62. Ellen Bass, "Our Stunning Harvest," *Reweaving the Web of Life: Feminism and Nonviolence*, pp. 63-72.
63. Barbara Deming, *We Are All Part of One Another*, p. 2.
64. Ibid., p. 203.
65. Marilyn French. *Beyond Power: On Women, Men, and Morals* (New York: Summit Books, 1985) p. 622.
66. Bahá'u'lláh, *Bahá'í World Faith*, p. 139.
67. Marilyn French, *Beyond Power*, p. 624.
68. From a line of a song by Linda Shear, "Family of Womyn."

Recommended Readings

Beyond Power: On Women, Men, and Morals, by Marilyn French (New York: Summit Books, 1985). An insightful analysis of the world's inequitable distribution of power. French demonstrates that patriarchy is neither natural, nor inevitable, and argues that we must embrace alternative human values (those considered feminine).

Learning to Live Without Violence, by Daniel Jay Sonkin and Michael Durphy (San Francisco: Volcano Press, 1982). A handbook for men to use in moving away from previously violent behaviors.

Reweaving the Web of Life: Feminism and Nonviolence, edited by Pam McAllister (Philadelphia: New Society Publishers, 1982). A collection of essays, poems, songs, photographs, stories dealing with the issues of feminism and nonviolence, as opposed to patriarchy and war.

We Are All Part of One Another: A Barbara Deming Reader, edited by Jane Meyerding with a foreword by Barbara Smith (Philadelphia: New Society Publishers, 1984). Four decades of writings by one of America's foremost activists in relation to civil rights, feminism, pacifism, and nonviolence.

Sisterhood is Global, edited by Robin Morgan (Garden City, New York: Anchor Books, 1984). A monumental anthology of the international women's movement, covering over sixty different countries.

Bahá'í Youth in the Peace Movement

by Karin Ryan Barnes

IT IS INCREASINGLY EVIDENT that the Bahá'í community is rapidly evolving to a new level of development, from even just a few years ago. Since the Universal House of Justice announced in 1985 that the Faith had emerged from obscurity, many changes can be observed in the way that Supreme Body has addressed the Bahá'ís in its correspondence, as well as in the types of events that occur on a regular basis within the community.[1] One significant event that marked an important step in that evolution was the letter from the Universal House of Justice dated October 20, 1983, which addressed the Bahá'í role in the social and economic development of humankind. This was a turning point for the community because, though all Bahá'ís knew that one day the Faith would move into that arena of activity, few had any idea that it would take such concrete form so soon.

The most recent in this succession of new directives from the Universal House of Justice is their peace statement addressed to the peoples of the world, released in October 1985. The significance of the letter is stated in its first paragraph:

The Great Peace towards which people of goodwill throughout the centuries have inclined their hearts, of which seers and poets for countless generations have expressed their vision, and for which from age to age the sacred scriptures of mankind have constantly held the promise, is now at long last within the reach of the nations. For the first time in history it is possible for everyone to view the entire planet, with all its myriad diversified peoples, in one perspective. World peace is not only possible but inevitable. It is the next stage in the evolution of this planet—in the words of one great thinker, "the planetization of mankind."

The question that many Bahá'ís have now is what activity to engage in that would best fulfill their duty to act out this new directive. For Bahá'ís are involved in a revolution: a peaceful, spiritual revolution. It is essential in any revolution to evaluate what sorts of activity must be undertaken to ensure its success. It is also important to evaluate the resources available to carry it out.[2]

One fundamental resource which always plays a significant role in every revolution is youth. Filled with enthusiasm, energy and idealism, it is very often they who dedicate themselves to progress and to work for a better future. This essay is devoted to the role of youth in the most significant social and economic development project of all time—world peace.

Active Involvement. How vital is it that the Bahá'í youth become involved in what is known as the peace movement? Not the Bahá'í community's efforts toward eventual peace, but the activities that take place outside the auspices of the Bahá'í community. A letter written on behalf of Shoghi Effendi reads:

The present conditions of the world—its economic instability, social dissensions, political dissatisfactions and international distrust—should awaken the youth from their slumber and make them enquire what the future is going to bring. It is surely they who will suffer most if some calamity sweep over the world. They should therefore open their eyes to the existing conditions, study the evil forces that are at play and then with a concerted effort arise and bring about the necessary reforms—reforms that shall contain within their scope the spiritual as well as social and political phases of human life.[3]

This statement affirms the active, not passive, role that Bahá'ís must play in those "phases of human life" which exist outside the direct control of the Bahá'í community. In a letter from the Universal House of Justice addressed to the Bahá'í youth of the world, dated January 3, 1984, a similar spirit is communicated:

The designation of 1985 by the United Nations as International Youth Year opens new vistas for the activities in which the young members of our community are engaged. The hope of the United Nations in thus focusing on youth is to encourage their conscious participation in the affairs of the world through their involvement in international development and such other undertakings and relationships as may aid the realization of their aspirations for a world without war.

The letter goes on:

Undoubtedly, it is within your power [referring to the youth] to contribute significantly to shaping the societies of the coming century; youth can move the world.[4]

In studying carefully the first statement, written on behalf of the Guardian, one is faced with some provocative issues. The letter states that the conditions of the world should " . . . awaken the youth from their slumber and make them enquire what the future is going to bring." Since the fate of humankind lies largely in the hands of its own members, one can only guess what lies directly ahead by observing and extrapolating trends and popular attitudes in an effort to determine what may occur if such trends and attitudes continue.

We observe that: increasingly the personal lives of many are in turmoil, racism is taking on new and more insidious dimensions, cities are terrorized by mass killers, nations are held hostage to war and starvation, governments cling to national sovereignty and their peoples to blind patriotism and nationalistic pride, the Superpowers are preparing for war—not just any war, but global thermonuclear war, the most imminent threat to the physical survival of the planet.[5] Though this threat is clearly a symptom of the larger disease from which humanity suffers—the disease of disunity and the perversion of true religion—it is no less serious in its implications. And the necessity of the whole-hearted attention of the Bahá'í community to this problem is no less essential.

The latter portion of the Guardian's statement suggests that the youth should " . . . open their eyes to the existing conditions," and that they should "study the evil forces that are at play." In order to make any significant contribution to progress, one must be informed about what one is trying to change. When the people refuse to become informed, it is difficult to bring about any change. For the adult population, this is the case with regard to the nuclear predicament. According to Robert Jay Lifton, M.D., professor of psychiatry at Yale University, most of the population is suffering from what he calls "psychic numbing": a defense mechanism which allows the individual to proceed with life's daily requirements without being overwhelmed by the precarious nature of the earth's continuing survival.[6]

Jonathan Schell, in his definitive analysis of the arms race and its implications, *The Fate of the Earth*, has written:

> Yet in spite of the immeasurable importance of nuclear weapons, the world has declined, on the whole, to think

about them very much. We have thus far failed to fashion, or to discover within ourselves, an emotional or intellectual or political response to them. This particular failure of response, in which hundreds of millions of people acknowledge the presence of an immediate, unremitting threat to their existence and to the existence of the world they live in but do nothing about it—a failure in which both self-interest and fellow-feeling seem to have died—has itself been such a striking phenomenon that it has to be regarded as an extremely important part of the nuclear predicament as this has existed so far.[7]

For the younger generation, it is very natural to acknowledge the significance, in terms of their own ability to understand, of such a predicament. According to Lonnie Carton, a Boston psychologist and family therapist, while most adults have learned to "keep preoccupied with success or making a living, the worry energy of children," unlike those of adults, has no release.[8] This fact in itself results in some harmful effects on children and youth.

In any case, once Bahá'í youth, following the directive of the Guardian, do open their eyes, look around, and make an attempt to "study the evil forces that are at play," it would be helpful to keep a few things in mind:

☐ It is essential that they remember that the Bahá'í writings have provided mankind with the necessary remedies for all the ills from which it suffers. Becoming hopelessly entangled in and perturbed by the human condition can only serve to harm the situation. It was the intention of the Guardian's statement to emphasize the need for this type of study in order to equip ourselves as Bahá'ís to bring about those "necessary reforms" through our life's activity, and so that we may be able to contribute to important, intelligent, and often times opinion-shaping conversations concerning world affairs.

☐ It is also important to acknowledge that the work of

the individual Bahá'í, as well as that of the community as a whole, can greatly reduce the suffering of humanity. The Universal House of Justice in its peace statement declared:

> Whether peace is to be reached only after unimaginable horrors precipitated by humanity's stubborn clinging to old patterns of behavior, or is to be embraced now by an act of consultative will, is the choice before all who inhabit the earth. At this critical juncture when the intractable problems confronting nations have been fused into one common concern for the whole world, failure to stem the tide of conflict and disorder would be unconscionably irresponsible.

Simply because Bahá'ís are aware of the ultimate solutions, this does not absolve them from responsibility for the work that must go on to (in the words of the Universal House of Justice) "improve the lot of man."[9] The differences of opinion that usually arise among Bahá'ís around this issue center around the question of "What exactly is the work we are called on to perform?"

☐ Our primary duty in carrying out Bahá'í activities is to carefully study and follow the directives of the Universal House of Justice. Their teaching plans provide the community with very concrete goals toward which to strive. Second are the activities that we are called on to participate in outside of the Bahá'í community. The Universal House of Justice has stated that:

> The time has come for the Bahá'í community to become more involved in the life of the society around it, without in the least supporting any of the world's moribund and divisive concepts, or slackening in its direct teaching efforts, but rather, by association, exerting its influence toward unity, demonstrating its ability to settle differences by consultation rather than by confrontation,

violence or schism, and declaring its faith in the divine purpose of human existence.[10]

Of course it is up to the individual, to a degree, to decide how to follow this course of action.

Education: In the latter part of the statement of the Guardian, it is suggested that the youth should "arise and bring about the necessary reforms—reforms that shall contain within their scope the spiritual as well as social and political phases of human life." Thus the activities of Bahá'í youth should extend not only to spiritual development (prayer, deepening, teaching, and attending the Nineteen-Day Feast) but they must somehow find a way to initiate necessary reforms in the social and political realms. The question is how? This author proposes that through mass education in the essential principles of peace, the oneness of humankind, collective security, international arbitration, and creative skills of consultation in resolving conflicts (among many others) all can participate in bringing humanity closer to global peace. It is stated in the peace statement of the House of Justice that: "In keeping with the requirements of the times, consideration should also be given to teaching the concept of world citizenship as part of the standard education of every child."

According to E. M. Rodgers, the rate of adoption of a new idea is as follows: when an innovative idea is introduced to the masses the rate of adoption is slow. In the beginning only small numbers of people accept the idea. However, once twenty percent of the population adopt any idea, it is unstoppable.[11] This concept is very useful when one begins to consider the importance and the logistics of educating humankind to these truths. It would then suggest that when twenty percent of the population of the world accepts the truth of humanity's oneness and of collective security, there will be an overwhelming call by people for the nations to unite and bring about world peace.

There are groups of people who are dedicated to this very occurrence. Beyond War, an organization dedicated to educating the public about these same principles, recently published full page ads in many of the nation's leading newspapers inviting the masses to participate in creating a world beyond war.[12] In Texas and in British Honduras, there are accredited schools that offer what is called a "world-core curriculum" authored by Robert Muller, United Nations assistant secretary general. As many as forty other nations have expressed interest in acquiring the curriculum as well. Gloria Buller, founder of the Robert Muller school at Arlington, says that the school "equips students to become planetary citizens."[13]

The Oneness of Humankind: In terms of educating youth in peace issues, there are two major principles which must be communicated: the organic oneness of humanity and the concept of collective security—the political unity of all nations. On June 24, 1982, the Bahá'í International Community addressed the Second Special Session of the United Nations General Assembly Devoted to Disarmament. It suggested "an extensive and intensive program of education of all peoples in the vital principle—and truth—of the organic oneness of humanity." They recommended "that such an educational program, with a universal curriculum adaptable to each culture, be fostered by governments, using schools, the media, businesses, industry, in fact all public and private means, in every country." It goes on further to state that "This program of education—drawing on all human knowledge bearing evidence to this oneness of humanity, whether from science or religion—would begin by fostering in all peoples an understanding and acceptance of the oneness of the human race, leading to an eventual acceptance of all the rich diversity of cultures as integral and unified elements of a single entity, and the recognition of the earth as the one home of the one human family."[14]

This concept of the organic oneness of the human race is not simply a pious notion that humanity will someday realize. It is a very real, tangible element that is working among all people every day—something that all of us participate in, whether or not we acknowledge its truth, everytime we interact with each other. It is something that every person on the face of the earth has the power to contribute to—and not someday, but NOW! It is a systematic, very practical way of eliminating those ethnocentric prejudices and superstitions which have led to such suffering and chaos and have kept humanity divided for so many years. What a service to humanity if such a curriculum could be implemented wherever possible.

The principle of the oneness of humanity is not only a truth that Bahá'ís are responsible for teaching to others, but it is a principle which Bahá'ís themselves, in many areas, must continually strive to attain. 'Abdu'l-Bahá said that:

In this way His Holiness Bahá'u'lláh expressed the oneness of humankind whereas in all religious teachings of the past, the human world has been represented as divided into two parts, one known as the people of the Book of God or the pure tree and the other the people of infidelity and error or the evil tree. The former were considered as belonging to the faithful and the others to the hosts of the irreligious and infidel; one part of humanity the recipients of divine mercy and the other the object of the wrath of their Creator. His Holiness Bahá'u'lláh removed this by proclaiming the oneness of the world of humanity and this principle is specialized in His teachings for He has submerged all mankind in the sea of divine generosity. Some are asleep; they need to be awakened. Some are ailing; they need to be healed. Some are immature as children; they need to be trained. But all are recipients of the bounty and bestowals of God.[15]

As Bahá'ís we, as a community, must understand that the suffering of each soul is our own suffering. If we do not try with our every effort to alleviate that suffering by bringing about the necessary changes in our world as soon as is humanly possible, we are missing perhaps the most significant aspect of the Bahá'í Revelation—human caring, being at one with the entire human race. It is not the intention of this author to suggest that Bahá'ís expend all of our efforts in treating symptomatic manifestations of the illness that the world is really suffering from. Nor is she suggesting that we, necessarily, should resort to traditional forms of protest, except as they may serve our purposes in particular instances. Nor is she trying to insist on an idea or a course of action that may be premature, and which may cause more harm than good.

It is clear that the teachings of Bahá'u'lláh provide the blueprint for the eventual peace of humanity. But to be singly concerned with the eventualities promised in the Faith is to ignore the needs of the here and now: the fact that our planet, our people, are facing the most extreme conditions of suffering ever known. And that our leaders, in the words of Shoghi Effendi: "in utter disregard of the spirit of the age, are striving to adjust national processes, suited to the ancient days of self-contained nations, to an age which must either achieve the unity of the world, as adumbrated by Bahá'u'lláh, or perish."[16]

If we can speed up the process by which the peoples of the world demand justice and the coming of age of their respective governments, this action would be a great service to humanity. Though the Bahá'í Writings state that the Bahá'í community will not directly cause the achievement of that political unity known as the Lesser Peace, individual Bahá'ís can have a tremendous effect on the events that shape our immediate future.

Collective Security and the Unity of Nations: In the writings of Bahá'u'lláh, 'Abdu'l-Bahá, and Shoghi Effendi are found many references to the inevitable political unification of the nations of the world. Bahá'u'lláh stated that this event would represent *"the world's Great Peace amongst men."*[17] Indeed the significance of this event cannot be overestimated, for it signals a complete reversal in the process of the disintegration of failing human institutions and the integration of new, world-embracing institutions. Such a shift in global attitude has not yet been witnessed by this ailing world. When the nations take this step, the direction of human endeavor will be altered forever, for when the nations cease spending hundreds of billions of dollars annually on weapons, how much more productive human achievement will become. Shoghi Effendi states that,

> Destitution on the one hand, and gross accumulation of ownership on the other, will disappear. The enormous energy dissipated and wasted on war, whether economic or political, will be consecrated to such ends as will extend the range of human inventions and technical development, to the increase of the productivity of mankind, to the extermination of disease, to the extension of scientific research, to the raising of the standard of physical health, to the sharpening and refinement of the human brain, to the exploitation of the unused and unsuspected resources of the planet, to the prolongation of human life, and to the furtherance of any other agency that can stimulate the intellectual, the moral, and spiritual life of the entire human race.[18]

In contrast to the intense suffering taking place around the globe, imagine how humanity would respond to the advent of such a world as the Guardian describes. It is a gift of inestimable value that must be offered to the world without hesitation. That is why this generation of youth and children must be instructed in the concept of collective security and international arbitration. For the masses are still heavily committed to a creed of nationalism that is destructive to this process of change. It must be demonstrated to the people of the world, particularly the youth, that the fruits of such a system of international unity would ensure them a future filled with progress and hope. The present systems can only ensure for them further suffering and, possibly, annihilation.

Empowerment: There is another very important aspect to the education of youth, *empowerment*. Empowerment is the acquisition of hope through social action. Recent studies have indicated that the youth and children of today are suffering from a sense of hopelessness and despair. In some cases this leads to immobilization as a result of intense fears of nuclear war.[19] Such fears in children have grown more intense over the past few years as a result of a growing awareness of the facts of our nuclear predicament; that is, the fact that it is highly unlikely that the earth, or at least its living organisms, would survive a global nuclear war.

Einstein once said, "I do not believe that we can prepare for war and at the same time prepare for a world community."[20] Yet regardless of the increasing body of facts that attest to the unsurvivability of such a disaster, our leaders continue to pursue a warlike policy in dealing with each other. Little wonder that children and youth envision nuclear war as inevitable. It is also understandable that they would lose the motivation to build a future for themselves.

The results of these studies have even been cited in recent legislation in California, the Vasconsellos Bill (AB 3848), which mandates peace studies in public schools. The purpose of this law was to acknowledge the current need for the public schools to deal specifically with nuclear issues and to find ways to empower youth to create a more healthy situation. That bill states that our children have indeed become immobilized because of our predicament and that "if left unchecked this lack of motivation and the feelings of helplessness could prove to be as devastating to American Society as war itself."[21] If the children have no hope for the future of the world because of the fear of global conflict, what will inspire them to plan for their own futures? What can convince them of the need to become educated and prepared to meet the challenges of adult life?

There must be a movement in the schools toward "empowerment training": education designed to inform today's youth of the conditions of human society, the causes of those conditions, and how their activities and concerns as individual members of a world community can alter those conditions. This program should combine with the teaching of the principles of the oneness of humanity and collective security because they are so interrelated.

The problem with many current attempts to educate youth about these issues is that they often communicate a lot of doom and gloom, with little or no emphasis on what can be done to alleviate the threat. This results in the frustration, depression, and immobilization of the youth. Though many dedicated individuals and organizations are working at remedying this, the public must show genuine concern for it to be integrated into the educational process. The second and third elements, namely the causes of our predicament and the role of individual initiative, must be integrated into such a program if we are to see any productive results.

Empowerment is the key. If this younger generation can be empowered to action through the investigation of facts surrounding these issues, they will surely reach the conclusion that the nations of the world must unite under a binding agreement in some form of representative world government, that all nations must be answerable to one law that protects the rights of every individual nation, and that there must be an international police force to protect its decisions. Otherwise ideological, religious, racial, and national disputes will ultimately result in the annihilation of the planet. This is a conclusion arrived at by world renowned figures. Einstein stated in 1946,

> Often in evolutionary processes a species must adapt to new conditions in order to survive. Today, the atomic bomb has altered profoundly the nature of the world as we

know it, and the human race consequently finds itself in a new habitat to which it must adapt its thinking.... In the light of new knowledge, a world authority and an eventual world state are not just desirable in the name of brotherhood, they are necessary for survival. In previous ages a nation's life and culture could be protected to some extent by the growth of armies in national competition. Today we must abandon competition and secure cooperation. This must be the central fact in all our considerations of international affairs; otherwise we face certain disaster. Past thinking and methods did not prevent world wars. Future thinking must prevent wars.[22]

Alvin Toffler, author of *Future Shock*, said in his more recent analysis of our world:

This new civilization, as it challenges the old, will topple bureaucracies, reduce the role of the nation-state, and give rise to semi-autonomous economies in a postimperialist world. It requires governments that are simpler, more effective, yet more democratic than any we know today. It is a civilization with its own distinctive world outlook, in its own way of dealing with time, space, logic, and causality.[23]

Jonathan Schell writes,

But if we accept both nuclear and conventional disarmament, then we are speaking of revolutionizing the politics of the earth. The goals of the political revolution are defined by those of the nuclear revolution. We must lay down our arms, relinquish national sovereignty, and found a political system for the peaceful settlement of international disputes.

He goes on to say that,

The task we face is to find a means of political action that will permit human beings to pursue any end for the rest of time. We are asked to replace the mechanism by which political decisions, whatever they may be, are reached. In sum, the task is nothing less than to reinvent politics: to reinvent the world.[24]

A Call to Action: The Universal House of Justice, in 1985, made this call to the masses of mankind: "Let men and women, youth and children everywhere recognize the eternal merit of this imperative action for all peoples and lift up their voices in willing assent. Indeed, let it be this generation that inaugurates this glorious stage in the evolution of social life on the planet."

So, what can we do outside of carrying out our daily obligations as Bahá'ís, such as teaching, praying and improving our characters, that will contribute to the cause of peace and bring it closer to reality? Of course there are many answers, depending on the individual and individual interests. All this author can offer is what she envisions as a practical means by which to achieve all of the suggestions set forth in this essay. The following is what she has already undertaken as such a means: In 1984 an organization was formed by a couple of Bahá'í youth who were very concerned with all the things spoken of here. They decided to name this organization Youth for World Peace, that it would not be a Bahá'í organization in name, but that it would be based on the fundamental principles of the Faith. Its major objectives were:

☐ To provide a meeting ground for people from all religions, races, political affiliations, classes, etc., where they could unite in one common cause: the cause of peace. If the organization were Bahá'í in name, there would be many who would not participate simply for that reason.
☐ To proclaim the verity of peaceful principles by

educating our own generation to our predicament and how we can do something to change it; to teach the significance and implications of the Bahá'í teachings themselves.

☐ To use 1985, International Youth Year, as a starting point for activities that will continue until our goal is achieved.

On January 31, 1985, the author received a letter from the Department of the Secretariat at the Bahá'í World Center written on behalf of the Universal House of Justice:

> The House of Justice is greatly pleased with the initiative you have taken with others to start an organization through which youth can contribute their considerable energies and creative abilities towards fostering world peace. It fully appreciates the wisdom of your approach in not affiliating your organization directly with the Faith and finds your leaflet describing the aims of Youth for World Peace most impressive. Since 1986 has been designated the International Year of Peace by the United Nations, your efforts are timely and will blend with the activities to be undertaken by the Bahá'í community during that year and beyond."[25]

This provided us with all the encouragement we needed. We proceeded to make plans for activities. The United Nations Association of San Diego agreed to sponsor our activities and provided tremendous support. The following is a description of the types of activities that have either already taken place, or are in the process of being planned.

☐ In November of 1984, two members of Youth for World Peace were invited to participate in a high school "Nuclear Awareness Week." The week was planned by one of the teachers at the school, who was also a member of Educators for Social Responsibility, and the representative from the Peace Resource Center of San Diego. The Y.W.P. representatives spoke to five groups of students about their organization and received a wonderful response. It opened their eyes to the receptivity of the young. We gained about one hundred new members.

□ In February of 1985, a symposium on world peace and disarmament was sponsored jointly by the United Nations Association of San Diego and Congressman Jim Bates, and coordinated by Youth for World Peace. The purpose of this gathering was to invite representatives from various organizations to give testimonials to be recorded, transcribed, and sent to the United Nations General Assembly and to the Congress.

□ In response to the urgency of dealing with children's fears of nuclear war, a monthly group seminar is planned for children and youth. A child therapist with a specialty in this area has agreed to volunteer his time once a month for this purpose.

□ A two week curriculum written by a Bahá'í has been approved to be implemented in the San Diego City School District as part of a new course entitled "World Government and Economics" which is now a requirement for all seniors in San Diego high schools. The social studies department for the San Diego City School District came to us, as we were working through the United Nations Association's Education Committee, and asked us to provide them with such a curriculum. The unit covers three main topics: factual data surrounding the nuclear predicament; the study of the interdependence of the world's nations; and the role of individual initiative in affecting change.

□ In November of 1985, Youth for World Peace presented a "World Economics Conference" directed at high school and college students interested in economics or political science. Its theme was world interdependence and how it is manifested through economic interrelationships among nations. The purpose of the conference was to interest students in a broader view of world economics and political relationships.

These are just a few of the activities the Y.W.P. is involved in. There are many others which we hope to participate in soon. One key activity that we are trying to promote is the formation of Peace Clubs in high schools and colleges all across the country. Through the establishment of these clubs, most of these activities can take place and a large number of youth can be reached. We need help. This is a grassroots effort and all talent is welcome.

References

1. The Universal House of Justice, Riḍván, 1985, To the Baha'ís of the World.
2. The Universal House of Justice, October 20, 1983.
3. From a letter dated March 13, 1932, written on behalf of Shoghi Effendi to an individual believer, quoted in *Bahá'í News*, no. 68 (Nov., 1932) p. 3.
4. The Universal House of Justice, quoted in *Unrestrained As the Wind* (Wilmette, Ill.: Bahá'í Publishing Trust, 1985) p. 183.
5. Ronald V. Dellums, *Defense Sense* (Cambridge, Mass.: Ballinger Publishing Company, 1983) p. xvii.
6. Quoted by Natalie Gittelson in "The Fear That Haunts Our Children," *McCall's Magazine* (May, 1982) p. 77.
7. Jonathan Schell, *Fate of the Earth* (New York: Alfred A. Knopf, 1982) p. 4.
8. Quoted by Natalie Gittelson in "The Fear that Haunts Our Children," p. 77.
9. The Universal House of Justice, October 20, 1983.
10. The Universal House of Justice, Riḍván 1985.

11. E. M. Rodgers and F. F. Shoemaker, *Communications of Innovations*, 1971; E. M. Rodgers, *Diffusion of Innovations*, 1983.

12. Beyond War, full page ad, *San Diego Union* (January 29, 1985) p. A-6. Also published in other papers nationwide.

13. Connie Zsweig, ed., "Planetary Curriculum accredited in Texas, spreads to British Honduras," *Leading Edge Magazine* (Sept. 24, 1984) p. 2.

14. The Bahá'í International Community, *Oral Statement to the Second Special Session of the United Nations on Disarmament*, June 24, 1982, New York.

15. 'Abdu'l-Bahá, *Bahá'í World Faith* (Wilmette, Ill.: Bahá'í Publishing Trust, 1943 [1976]) p. 246.

16. Shoghi Effendi, *Call to the Nations*, (Haifa: Bahá'í World Centre, 1977) p. 21.

17. Bahá'u'lláh, *Gleanings from the Writings of Bahá'u'lláh*, (Wilmette, Ill.: Bahá'í Publishing Trust, 1939 [1971]) p. 249.

18. Shoghi Effendi, *The World Order of Bahá'u'lláh* (Wilmette, Ill.: Bahá'í Publishing Trust, 1938 [1974]) p. 204.

19. Beardsly, Mack, *The Impact of Nuclear Developments on Children and Adolescents*, A.P.A.'s Task Force Report, #20.

20. Albert Einstein, "Only Then Shall We Find Courage," *New York Times Magazine* (June 23, 1946).

21. Vasconsellos, *Nuclear Age Education Curriculum, AB 3848*, Sept. 29, 1984, California State Legislative Council Section 51755 d.

22. Albert Einstein, "Only Then Shall We Find Courage."

23. Alvin Toffler, *The Third Wave* (New York: William Morrow Co., 1980) p. 25.

24. Jonathan Schell, *Fate of the Earth*, p. 226.

25. Department of the Secretariat, The Universal House of Justice, January, 31, 1985.

A Bahá'í Goes to War

by David Langness

When Kalimát Press asked me to write an essay about peace for this book, I reflected on my twenty years in the peace movement, selected a suitably elevated, intellectual topic, and then proceeded to expound. After a few weeks, producing another theory-laden think-piece about ways to achieve a world free of war began to seem like a futile exercise. There are hundreds of great essays on peace. I knew that nothing I could write would even come close to the eloquence of 'Abdu'l-Bahá's simplest informal talk on the subject. So I threw out what I had written (it was terrible) and decided to write about something very personal instead, something I had never written about before, something that I suspect many Bahá'ís have never read about.

This essay, then, is about my war. Like war, it is obscene. I write about war in a book about peace because I believe that to truly work for peace, one must understand what happens in its absence. Because of the nature of this essay, children should not read it. No adult who is deeply offended by foul language or descriptions of human depravity should read it. These words were written not to shock or offend, but to accurately record the experiences of one Bahá'í who went to war and returned to tell about it. I apologize in advance to those readers who will take umbrage at what follows. But I suggest multiplying the offense felt by a factor of several thousand, and then applying the resultant outrage to the elimination of the conditions that make such profoundly offensive human behavior possible.

I thank you for your tolerance.

"TAKE IT, YOU STUPID peacenik maggot bastard!"

I was looking up at a shiny new M-16 automatic assault rifle, an Army drill sergeant, and two of his buck sergeant cohorts from where I sat on the asphalt. My head spun. The Fort Ord, California sun shone down on all of us, warm and golden even in early spring. My mouth was bleeding, and I kept wiping it off with my hand, hoping none would drip on my fatigues. Bloodstains were impossible to get out, and if they stayed in it meant more KP, more pushups, more cleaning latrines. I'd already had enough of that.

"Damn pinko pervert," one of the buck sergeants screamed at me. Only twelve weeks ago I would have sworn nobody could utter that kind of vintage Joe McCarthy cartoon dialogue with a straight face, much less believe it. But he screamed it again, his face contorted with rage and hatred. All one hundred twenty men in the infantry training company I had been assigned to looked on from a short distance, most equally angry, some quiet, a few secretly sympathetic.

"I *ordered* you to pick up this weapon, private maggot!" It was the drill sergeant again, his flat-brimmed Smokey-the-Bear hat waggling on his shaved head as he held the M-16 at arm's length and tried to force me to take it. Blood and tissue from my face dripped off the black plastic stock that he had butt-stroked me to the ground with a minute ago.

"No, sergeant," I answered, loudly.

"You *will* pick up this weapon and train with it like you

got a pair of balls, fag!" It was the other buck sergeant yelling this time.

I sat on the asphalt and said nothing.

"Are you refusing a direct order, Langness?!"

"I'm a conscientious objector, sergeant," I explained again. "No direct order can make me pick up a weapon. The Selective Service and the Army gave me C.O. status, and that means I don't kill people or train to kill people."

"You are a miserable damn excuse for a soldier, private puke," the drill sergeant shouted, spittle flying from his mouth and landing on my face. "I'm going to personally guaran-damn-tee you get your sorry chickens--t ass shipped to Vietnam, where we'll sure as hell see if this goddamn conscientious objector crap does you any f--king good. I hope Charlie kills your cowardly ass thirty ways from Sunday. Now get out of my sight."

The three of them made smart about-faces and left me on the parade ground. "Damn," I said, looking down. There was blood on my fatigues, and that meant I'd have to buy another pair.

At seventeen, I had been around Bahá'ís for a couple of years. After the inevitable early teenage agnosticism, I'd investigated Buddhism, Zen and its various permutations, and several others, but the unique Bahá'í mix of mysticism and reason seemed to make the most sense. I'd go to meetings, firesides, proclamations, bring my friends. Then Bob Habermann and I—the two holdouts—would hang around outside of Feast waiting for the social portion, drinking a beer or two, shooting some pool, and telling each other how glad we were not to have to belong to an organized religion like our friends inside.

At first, I was attracted to Bahá'ís and their faith primarily for political reasons. At fourteen I'd gone to my first CORE and NAACP meetings, and soon found myself committed to the civil rights movement. I'd march, sit in, go for coffee, write letters to editors, stuff envelopes, anything to help. But even at that age I could begin to see that those things weren't working. When Malcolm X was killed, they seemed to work even less. So it was the young blood of the movement—Stokely Carmichael and Rap Brown and the burning intellect of Julius Lester—that appealed to me. They were saying, with increasing fervor, that the system ought to be torn down, not patched up.

And the war, of course, couldn't be ignored. For a rebellious white kid who hung out in coffeehouses and around the the beats, my natural inclination was toward disarmament, peace, world unity. It helped that my father had been a famous World War II Marine hero, repeatedly decorated, field commissioned, ticker tape parades—the man the Marines sent to Hollywood to teach John Wayne how to get it right—because he hated every slogan I mouthed and every peace-related cause I espoused, which of course gave me a happy and newly minted sense of personal autonomy and freedom that was exhilarating.

So for several years, nonviolence and peace were my central focus. And slowly, instead of being the gopher, I began to lead. Organizing demonstrations, vigils, silent candlelight marches, giving talks, speeches, harangues; quoting the obligatory Gandhi and Gibran and Marcuse, working on committees, brotherhood workshops, and on and on. My own commitment, I felt, was just a small contribution compared to that of most of the people working for peace and social justice, who paid with their entire lives, sometimes literally. It didn't take long to become jaded, either, because the inflexibility of the system was overwhelming. It gave only in token amounts, it seemed, and never really changed fundamentally. Rosa Parks was riding in the front of the bus, but she was still riding to the same rotten job that wouldn't feed her kids.

Then along came S.D.S.—Students for a Democratic Society. They wouldn't let us white boys join the Panthers and the peace-loving turn-the-other-cheek attitude was slowly proving untenable for the impatient, and even for some of the patient, so S.D.S. was wonderful. S.D.S. would do just about anything, which was liberating, fun, crazy, intense. Occupy the dean's office. Pour cow's blood on the Dow Chemical recruitment table. Chant "Hell, no, we won't go!" (pretty racy after "We Shall Overcome"). The war was evil, the ultimate evil, and we were an absolute moral force, ready to fight it with everything we had. But that began to include a few things I wasn't real comfortable with—Molotovs, Mace, helmets, and sticks.

Then Bob decided to become a Bahá'í, leaving me in the lurch. "I couldn't resist anymore," he told me. "It made so much sense." My friends, my own brother, everyone I knew and respected was signing a declaration card and walking around all smiles. I resisted the peer pressure. "Come on, you gotta do it," Ron Drossman told me urgently after he'd signed his card. "What are you waiting for?"

So at seventeen, two huge decisions loomed—the draft and Bahá'u'lláh. And they were inextricably intertwined. My local draft board had never approved a conscientious objector request. But by that time one thing was clear to me—that I would never, no matter what, kill another human being. And Bahá'u'lláh influenced me more than anyone else I read, with *"It is better to be killed than to kill."*

The conundrum was this: if I got drafted and couldn't get the conscientious objector status I wanted, they'd put a gun in my hand and order me to kill. If I became a Bahá'í I'd have some help getting the C.O. status (Bahá'ís were granted it almost as a matter of course, I was told). But I was almost sure to get drafted (the C.O.s were drafted first). And there was the fight between my soul—attracted immensely to the spiritual truths and the social principles of the Bahá'í Faith—and my mind, which told me constantly that I shouldn't limit myself to a singular point of view, even one as seemingly broad and universal as the Bahá'ís'. So if I dodged the draft by going to Canada, or sliming my way out, or staying in the university solely for sanctuary, it all amounted to the same thing—which was not facing up to the hard moral choice. And if I believed in anything then, it was facing the hard choices.

So I became a Bahá'í. It was the first time I ever let the innermost part of my being—my essential spiritual core—make a major decision. For that reason, it felt right—I was letting my instincts have their head, which was like signaling to the horse you're riding that he should run as far and as fast as he can. The morning of my eighteenth birthday, I filled out the old dog-eared declaration card that had been stuck in my prayer book for three years and took it to my friend Frank's house and gave it to him. He was wreathed in smiles, happy as could be, and he insisted that we immediately drive it over to the Local Spiritual Assembly secretary's house, so it would be official. When we got there, she took one look at the card, scowled at my long hair and old jeans, and said to Frank, "Oh, no, not another one." Later we laughed again and again at the memory of her reception, but that day it wasn't funny.

On the same day I filled out my draft registration form, an act that I remember clearly because it was actually physically painful for me to write my name on that innocuous card. "What the hell are you doing?" I asked myself over and over. The clerk smiled happily. One day, two signatures. I prayed I was doing the right thing.

I applied for the noncombatant draft status called 1-AO, which meant that you would serve in the Army, but not be trained to kill or required to bear arms. They called 1-AO a noncombatant status, but that was an ugly misnomer—because most C.O.s served in combat, trying to save the wounded. 1-AO's were trained as medics, and almost all went to Vietnam, where they were needed. As C.O.s, they carried no weapons. A medic's life expectancy in the field in Southeast Asia was the shortest of all combat jobs, and it got even shorter without a way to defend yourself. There was one other C.O. classification, called 1-O, which meant you weren't drafted at all. Instead you were required to perform some type of alternative civic service, like working in a hospital for two years at low pay. That one I didn't apply for: "Impossible to get," everyone had told me, "and besides, the Bahá'ís should obey their governments and show that they are willing to serve, just not to kill." Six months later, after three appeals, the final one to President Nixon, the Selective Service System agreed to make me a bonafide conscientious objector. When the presidential decision came one day in the mail, I was happy that they finally appreciated the seriousness of my commitment—but I knew the classification was my ticket to war.

So on Bahá'u'lláh's birthday, November 12, 1969, I was inducted into the United States Army. The Army that I had railed against in the peace movement for five long years had claimed me, because Bahá'u'lláh asked that I obey my government and do as they ordered. My feelings were horribly mixed. I wanted to follow the teachings of my new Faith, but a part of me despised everything the Army stood for—nationalism, rule by violence, killing as foreign policy, forced conscription—and yet here I was, in uniform, in the belly of the beast. I consoled myself with thoughts of becoming a medic and tried to bury my anguish by reaffirming my commitment to saving lives instead of taking them. And the night before, my Bahá'í friends brought me a new prayer book and I asked each of them to sign it.

On induction day in Phoenix most of us took the oath. You signified that you would "defend the honor of your country against enemies domestic and foreign" by taking one step forward. The ones who didn't step forward went to prison for refusing to do their duty for their country. There were about a hundred of us in the induction center that day, and thirty did not take the step. I wanted not to—badly. I took it only on the tenuous thread of my new belief in an obscure nineteenth-century Persian prophet named Bahá'u'lláh, and his principle of obedience to a duly-constituted government. I had serious, deep questions still. But on that day the collective answer to them was obviously yes.

The Army despises conscientious objectors. They took us, but only because the civilian-run Selective Service forced them to. The Army singles C.O.s out, trains them in the worst possible conditions, subjects them to brutality and harassment, does everything it can to change their minds, and generally makes life even more miserable than it does for the normal draftee. Being a lover of peace inside the engine of war is no picnic.

It started with the ritual of homogenization and dehumanization that the Army deems best to train its soldiers. Everything yours was taken from you. No clothes, jewelry, watches, wallets—nothing personal was left. Your hair was shaved off. You were given olive drab fatigues that purposely didn't fit, boots that were too small, and dog tags that had your name, serial number, blood type and religious affiliation. I raised my hand in the huge hall where we filled out the papers for dog tag issue, because the Bahá'í Faith wasn't included in the list of 99 religious preferences on the wall.

"Speak, dog turd!" the big, sadistic-looking PFC who ran the place screamed at me.

"Uh, I . . ."

"Sound off, dog turd!" You had to scream back if you wanted to be heard.

"I don't see my religion up there, private."

"That's Private First Class Norman to you, dog turd!" Colorful nicknames for the new recruits were part of the fun.

"I don't see my religion up there, Private First Class Norman."

"And just what is your religion, candy ass?!"

"Bahá'í, Private First Class Norman."

"Ba-what?!" There was laughter in the room.

"Bahá'í—the Bahá'í Faith."

"You those wimps with the towels around they heads, maggot?!"

"No, sir."

"Don't call me sir, maggot. I'm an enlisted man! I work for a living!"

"What do you suggest I put down, then, Private First Class Norman?"

"YOU MOCKING ME BOY?!" He dropped the skin magazine he'd been perusing and stood up out of his chair, glaring.

"No."

"Put 'No Preference,' s--thead."

"I don't want to put 'No Preference.' I have a preference, and it's the Bahá'í, *bee, ay, aych, ay, apostrophe eye,* Faith." I was angry.

"I SAID PUT NO PREFERENCE, YOU S--T-FOR-BRAINS!!"

After I did that he ordered me to do fifty pushups. Insubordination, he said.

A few months later, I had a friend in personnel make me a dog tag that said "BAHA I" on the religious preference line. The Army didn't have apostrophes.

For basic training we were segregated from all other soldiers and sent to a special conscientious objector unit at Fort Sam Houston in San Antonio, Texas. This was done, as far as we could determine, for two reasons—to keep our seditious political views away from the gung-ho soldiers who *wanted* to kill; and to subject us to the absolute worst the Army had to offer.

For C.O. basic at Fort Sam, the Army detailed its meanest, nastiest drill sergeants. Many had records of violence and brutality against trainees in regular basic training units, so the Army hid them away at Fort Sam, where they could operate virtually unnoticed. We were a small, anonymous unit, out of the mainstream, housed in five buildings that had been constructed soon after the American defeat at the Alamo.

"You Seventh Day Adventist, or Christian?" the drill sergeant asked me when I arrived. He had a list with two columns and he was putting each trainee's name in one or the other.

"Neither, drill sergeant," I said proudly, "I'm a Bahá'í."

"Good!" he smiled widely. "That means you can work on Saturdays *and* Sundays, asshole."

A typical day at Fort Sam Houston went like this:

Up at four, when the drill sergeants ran through the barracks screaming obscenities at the tops of their lungs and banging on the metal bunks with swagger sticks and baseball bats. Their names for us ranged from the completely crude to the nastily creative, but most were some derogatory variation on the street slang for different parts of the female anatomy, or various suggestions of homosexuality. Manhood, theirs and ours, was always the issue. "After all," one drill sergeant in a kindly, explanatory mood once told us, "how can you have a working pair of testicles and not want to kill gooks?"

Then it was out to formation, where roll call and a four-mile run at close-order ranks in combat boots through the pre-dawn darkness started the day. We would be ordered to sing marching songs, called jody-counts, as we ran:

I wanna lead a life of danger.
I wanna go to Vietnam.
I wanna be an Airborne Ranger.
I wanna kill some Viet Cong.

Meals were rushed through to make time for hours of PT, an exercise/torture session hilariously called physical therapy, and hours of marching on a parade field called D and C, or drill and ceremony. We learned to take orders immediately without questioning—"Save your life in the 'Nam some day, germs"—to function on no sleep and total physical exhaustion, to force-march seventeen miles with a forty pound pack in a day, to be attacked by tear gas and shot at with live machine-gun ammo, to be made to do fifty or a hundred or a thousand pushups or sit-ups on the angry whim of a sergeant or anyone else, and to take it all without complaint. We would spend six hours in the middle of the night buffing the barracks floor to a mirror shine, only to have a drill sergeant come in and grind dirt and shoe polish and laundry detergent into the wax and command us to do it again.

In between the physical training came the classes—films from the forties on avoiding venereal disease; how to use the Army's entrenching tool (insert in ground, dig, dispose of dirt, insert in ground . . .); lectures on the evil specter of communism and the domino theory; memorization of the chain of command and repeated quizzes on same:

"Langness!"

"Yes, sir!"

"Who is the Secretary of the Army?"

"Donald Resor, sir!"

"That's correct, troop. Who is the Under-Secretary of the Army?"

"Uh, I don't know, sir."

"You sleeping in my classes, dickbreath?"

"No, sir. I was on KP that day."

"Get down and give me fifty, and I don't want to hear any more of your pussy excuses, you rodney." A rodney, like a cherry or a FNG, was the dumb newcomer.

This went on for six weeks. At night, when you were so tired you climbed into your rack with your boots and fatigues still on, the usual subject of after lights-out discussion was the abnormal level of sadism of one or another drill sergeant, the unfairness of the Army, the rotten food, or some variant of "Boy, I'll be glad when I get out of here." Rarely did it turn to philosophizing about war or the nature of man or any of the higher, more spiritual forms of discourse. Most kept their thoughts to themselves, few talked about the stands they had taken or the costs of taking them. But all acted out their ideals in the face of massive opposition. In a group like this, I came to discover, the private moral choices each man had made were his alone, usually driven inside by the pressure to conform and obey. His actions, though, were the measure of his convictions. That anyone can make a stand for an abstract principle in the face of such pressure was for me a signal of victory of the human spirit, and I took a battered body and mind out of basic training with the aid of a new spiritual strength that surprised me.

In about the fifth week of the Fort Sam ordeal, an officer came around to interview all of us. Coincidentally, he was the brother of one of the friends I'd made there. I'll call him Carl, for reasons that will become obvious.

Carl was a member of the C.I.D., or criminal investigation division, of the Army. A clandestine, secret, feared group, the C.I.D. is the Army's own FBI and CIA combined, with massive powers and almost unlimited funding and manpower. We learned after the first interview that Carl, although friendly toward us because of his brother, was asking questions about our political activities before the Army. We had no idea why.

When I went in to see Carl, he already knew who I was.

"Hi," he said pleasantly, "my brother tells me you're one of the good guys." He was sitting behind a desk, and I took a chair.

"And here I thought he was pretty astute," I said. Carl laughed. He had a thick manila file folder in front of him.

"I'm here to talk to all you people about your beliefs and your political activities, just for informational purposes. Private Langness, you've got the thickest file of anyone." He patted the sheaf of documents. My eyes were riveted on the folder, amazed.

"Will you answer a few questions for me, then?"

"Sure," I said.

"Have you ever advocated the overthrow of the United States Government?"

"Yup."

"The violent overthrow?" He seemed surprised.

"That's a tougher one," I said.

"O.K. Have you ever taken any violent measures against the government?"

"Myself?"

"Yes."

"No—I wanted to, but no."

"Why not?"

"Well, when I was in S.D.S., I just couldn't bring myself to do it. Basic nonviolent tendencies, I suppose. Once in a while I carried the bombs, but I never threw one. Then, I became a Bahá'í about a year ago. You know what that is?"

"Uh-uh," he said, taking notes.

"Well, the Bahá'ís believe in the emergence of one world government. And we're committed to nonviolence, to peace. That's why I'm here, instead of bombing draft boards."

He looked up at me. "Good," he said. "Hey, will you wait here for ten minutes? I'm going to see my brother for ten minutes, then I'll be back." He grinned at me. This was strange—the first time any ranking Army man had ever treated me respectfully. He walked out, and there I sat with my file folder still on the desk in front of me. It took me a while to realize why he had said "ten minutes" twice. When I did, I got up fast and had a look.

The folder held all kinds of documents and memos, which I didn't have time to read. I skimmed them quickly. But it also had pictures—literally dozens of glossy, eight-by-ten black-and-white shots of me in demonstrations, in meetings, coming out of my house and other people's homes, even one of a girlfriend and me in a line for a movie. The pictures shocked me profoundly—seeing myself in government photos that I didn't know were being taken. Finding this thick file with records of my movements, the demonstrations and the meetings and the study groups and even some of the

Bahá'í firesides I had attended, was deeply disturbing. It confirmed the paranoia that all of us who fought to change things already felt. In ten minutes Carl came back with a smile and told me I was free to go. I detected a little irony in his tone.

From basic training we all went to another part of the base to undergo the Army's ten-week version of medical school. We would emerge as qualified medics, who would be able, theoretically, to treat the most grievous of war injuries. A huge sign on the side of the medic training building said: "So the wounded may live to fight another day." Not exactly what I had in mind, I thought.

The training was thorough, learning to apply immediate life-saving medicine that would allow us to get G.I.s out on the medevac chopper and to the physicians in the evacuation hospitals as quickly as possible. "Vietnam has the lowest level of injury deaths of any war," they told us, "because those helicopters really save lives." The level of harassment was somewhat reduced now that we were no longer basic trainees, but each week brought all of us closer to Vietnam. Rumors persisted. "We're all going to Germany," or "We're staying stateside," were the optimistic ones. Our company first sergeant dashed all that in week seven when he called us into formation, held up a single sheet of orders and, with a fulsome grin, gleefully announced, "Every swingin' dick to ROV!"—Republic of Vietnam. There was total silence. I looked around and knew, statistically, that the majority of us (average age: nineteen) wouldn't live through the next year. The fact lodged in my throat like a sharp bone.

But in week nine, when we were close to graduation, I was called aside by the company clerk.

"Orders," he told me, handing me a sheaf of papers.

"Langness, David E.," they said, "report immediately to Fourth Replacement Company, Ford Ord, California." That was it. There was no explanation.

"What?" I asked him. "With one week to go? Why?" I was filled with relief and some shame, because I was now going to California and because every one of my new friends was going to war.

The company clerk looked over both of his shoulders before he spoke.

"Carl." He explained in a whisper. "You're a subversive."

At Fort Ord things got tough. The replacement company turned out to be a holding company for every manner of Army misfit, and I was just added to the pile. It was the first time I'd been around the actual Army, not just housed with fellow C.O.s. Soldiers with lost files, indeterminate assignments, those with just a few days or weeks left, people too sick to work but too healthy to be hospitalized, and a few like me, consigned into a kind of bureaucratic limbo because the Army didn't really know what to do with us. We were presided over by an ill-tempered staff sergeant who sent us on various details of military importance like picking up the base's never-ending supply of cigarette butts, cleaning the general's wife's storage closets, raking sand, painting curbs, etc. One day we double-timed out to the firing range at Fort Ord's beautiful beach and spent ten hours digging and burying three million dollars worth of ammunition that a supply captain had mistakenly ordered. Then, when the staff sergeant realized after three or four weeks of details that I was a conscientious objector, the trouble started.

"Hey, you, Langness," he called me over one day.

"Yes, sergeant."

"You 1-AO?"

"Sure am."

"You little prick." His grin turned ugly, and he put his hand on my chest and shoved me backwards out of his office.

The next day my new orders came. Eleven Bravo, they said, which was the assignment every draftee feared the most—infantryman. Ground pounder. Foot soldier. Grunt.

They were sending me to train to be a killer. I was outraged and enraged, but every avenue of appeal that I tried led nowhere. I determined to resist.

That meant two weeks of getting beat up, in the end. I'd refuse to pick up the weapon, and they'd have fits. They'd argue, order, fume, punch and kick me, scream. I'd refuse some more. They'd send me back to the holding company, and the holding company sergeant would send me to another eleven bravo training unit somewhere else on the post, where the pattern would be repeated. We went around that mulberry bush six times, with six different companies.

I tried to get in to see ranking officers, but was refused. I called the local draft counseling center in Monterey, and they told me to come in, that what the Army was doing—trying to assign a conscientious objector to a combat job—was illegal and qualified me for immediate release from the service. But there was no way I could get off the base. My antagonist the staff sergeant kept assigning me to new details, cleaning out kitchen grease traps, waking me in the middle of the night for guard duty, swamping out the motor pool's filthy garages, anything demeaning he could think of. Once I heard him bragging to other sergeants that he was going to hound me until I broke and deserted, which meant I'd land in some federal pen where people like me belonged.

Finally I went to see the base Colonel early one morning, unannounced. I sat on his doorstep until his chauffeur brought him in.

"Sir, can I see you for a moment?"

He was flustered, because this was not standard operating procedure, but he had some warmth and kindness around his eyes. He invited me in.

I explained, and he looked very disturbed. He kept staring at the cuts and bruises on my face.

"What would you like to do in the Army, son?" he finally asked.

I told him I didn't know enough about the Army to know, but that I'd do anything as long as I didn't have to kill people.

"Can you type?" he wondered. When I told him yes, he said, "Good. We'll make you a company clerk."

The next day I was a company clerk. In a small training unit for Army communications wiremen, who we called pole-climbers because that's what they did, I sat in the company headquarters office and kept records, typed correspondence, and filled out forms. This was comparative heaven: I had a room to myself, worked in a reasonable environment, and had weekends off. Nobody ordered me to pick up a weapon or brutalized me when I didn't. I was astonished at my good fortune. It lasted for two months.

Then orders came again, delivered in the same fashion—without warning or explanation. This time for Fort Rucker, Alabama, to Army air traffic controller school—a complete mystery to everyone, especially my company commander, who tried hard to keep me at Ord, but to no avail. In a week, I was in the Deep South at yet another base, mystified as to why the Army didn't want "subversives" like me treating their wounded and getting shot at but did want us controlling million-dollar aircraft and the people who flew them.

Air traffic control school was intensive and long—four months—and I was the first C.O. to ever go through. The benefit was teaching the Faith in the South on weekends, when I'd go out with Bahá'ís from Atlanta or Montgomery and walk into the dusty rural counties that were such fertile fields for waiting souls. On one excursion into Bogalusa, Louisiana, however, a young black Bahá'í girl and I were thrown into jail for the heinous crime of walking down the street together. Four policemen, probably all Klan members, slapped us around and interrogated us for five hours.

"What's it like to sleep with a nigger, boy?"

"You people civil rights workers?"

"We killed King, and we're gonna kill the likes of you, too, coons."

"Nigger-lovers ain't welcome around hyeah, boy."

After that Saturday I found myself actually enjoying the relative security of an Army post again—until Monday, when my orders for Vietnam came.

At the staging base outside of Saigon, we were assigned our units. The sergeant walked past me, then came back, studying me and my personnel folder. We stood outside in formation in the unbelievable tropical heat and humidity, a hundred and fifteen, at ninety percent, the Southeast Asian version of a nice day.

"Just what the hell is yo' MOS, PFC Langness?" the assignment sergeant asked. "This damn folder says you got about fo' of 'em."

An MOS is your military occupational specialty—your job. Unlike most draftees, my stateside career had been varied, and I had several MOSs listed. I'd even become a little smug at that point, because I'd been in the Army almost a year now and because I knew that air traffic controllers were always assigned to relatively safe rear areas, sitting in air-conditioned buildings, directing pilots.

"That's right, Sarge," I chuckled. "Medic, clerk, what have you, now an air traffic controller. It's been a hell of a ride."

"You ain't seen nothin' yet, G.I.," he chuckled back amiably, putting a check mark on a form that bore my name, "cause you about to go up-country where da wah is and doctor for the Hundred and First Airborne. Chuck that other s--t. The One-oh-worst be needin' medics in the worse kinda way." He strolled on down the line of soldiers, his feet kicking up little clouds of dust, and left me stunned for a second. Then, for some reason, I started to laugh hysterically. Others in the formation backed away a little warily.

"Fool's crazy," somebody said. "Goin' upcountry to die, and laughin' 'bout it." I laughed so hard my sides hurt.

"Where da wah is" was no lie. The 101st Airborne division had a reputation for taking on the most dangerous and difficult assignments, and they had certainly done so in Vietnam. Famous for its battles in the European theater during World War II, the 101st was assigned to duty in South Vietnam's dreaded I Corps, which was the region bordering the Demilitarized Zone (the DMZ) and Cambodia. In other parts of the country, any soldier with the 101's shoulder patch—a Screaming Eagle in full color, disdainful of the Army command that all insignia be black and green for camouflage purposes—was generally feared and respected. That was because the war was fought the hardest and heaviest in what they called Eye Core, and the soldiers who went there did not come back unchanged, or they simply did not come back.

My new unit—a little company of 101st Airborne grunts that operated in the hills and western jungles of I Corps— was to be home for the next eight months. Far away from the large cities of the region like Hue and Da Nang, we learned to live in the jungle, eat cold C-rations, sleep in shallow foxholes, kill the Viet Cong and be killed by the Viet Cong. I was the medic, so I patched up the wounded, counseled the disturbed, tried to lead my life by spiritual principles in the midst of their antithesis, turned twenty-one in an open bunker while pinned down by rocket and mortar fire, and bagged the dead.

"Say, doc." Every medic was called doc.

"Say, Henry." Henry was the M-60 man, the one who carried the machine gun. It was my first week on the job.

"Can you look at this deal?" Without waiting for me to answer, Henry rolled up his pant leg and showed me a huge, ulcerated open wound on his shin. It was eaten through by maggots, and some bone showed.

"How'd that happen?" I asked him as I took the antibiotic-filled syringe out of my kit and sponged off the disgusting white larval bugs and the dirt with alcohol.

"Leeches," Henry said. "Rice paddies're full of 'em."

"Why didn't you burn the leech off, or use your bug juice before if got so bad?" I was the new guy, but even I knew no one had to let leech bites get that infected.

"Hell, doc." Henry looked at me like I was a mental defective.

"It's pretty bad, buddy," I told him, shaking my head, still not getting it. "You shouldn't be walking on it. I'm going to give you some of this antibiotic and send you out of here tomorrow morning on the medevac chopper."

"All-*right*!" Henry said, dancing away gleefully before I had a chance to finish the bandage.

For the first several weeks after I arrived, we never saw a single VC—but we were eaten alive by their booby traps. Pungi stakes, which were sharpened pieces of wood set upright in the ground and covered with excrement to promote instant infection, went through boot and foot immediately if you stepped in the wrong place. The Bouncing Betty was a little spring-loaded grenade in a can that jumped up from the ground when you tripped it, to explode at face or solar plexus level. Pressure-release mines were used everywhere, and they were diabolical because they went off when you stepped off them instead of on, so they were called heel-poppers. Command-detonated mines were laid in the trail and set off when your platoon was right over them, usually by a sniper in a nearby tree or tunnel. It was almost always the point man or number two that set off the booby trap, though, since they were first through an area, so the column would stop and I'd hear the call of "Medic! Medic up!"

I hated that call. It meant there was somebody I knew writhing on the ground, his midsection or his face blown apart, his feet or his groin or his legs mangled, and that I was responsible for seeing to it that he lived. I'd run to the front of the column, try to get the bleeding stopped, try to prevent the worst effects of the shock, try to stabilize the vital signs so he'd have enough time—usually twenty minutes or so—to get on the medevac chopper and be flown to the evacuation hospital. I would do these things almost automatically, all the while trying to soothe and comfort the kid from a farm in Oklahoma or a ghetto in Bedford-Stuyvesant with lying reassurances that everything was going to be all right. Sometimes the booby trap would get two or three or four of these hapless teenagers, and I'd have to rush from one to the other tying off gushing arteries, plugging sucking-chest wounds, doing a quick emergency tracheotomy or splinting a compound fracture while pumping in the painkillers. And then, if our luck ran out, I'd run low on supplies, we'd come under fire, or it would be so dark and rainy that the helicopters couldn't get in. And there I would be with a couple of dying eighteen-year-olds, their pleading eyes and the eyes of their friends on me. I held them when they died, and each of their deaths made me angrier and crazier.

"Medic up!"

I ran through the dense triple-canopy jungle to the front again, after the explosion. It was Brubaker and Hanh, the Vietnamese scout. Both were shredded with shrapnel from a homemade Chicom grenade that had been packed around its circumference with scrap metal from old U.S. C-ration cans Army boys had left lying around the jungle. The VC took perverse delight, it sometimes seemed, in killing us with our own litter. Hanh was nearly dead, and there was nothing I could do for him, so I tended to Brubaker. Triage, as the cynical saying went, is a bitch.

It was getting dark, and the lieutenant who was leading our little patrol for three days on this mission came up to talk to me while I worked.

"Hey, doc," he said, "how long?"

"He's cut up pretty bad, and there's one intestinal wound, but he'll make it if we can get him out," I reported. "Only thing is, we've had so damn many of these things I'm running out of painkillers. If we could . . ."

Just then there was a sound like a swarm of bees buzzing through the leafy jungle. I looked up from where I found myself in the dirt, and it was only then I heard the pop-pop-popping of our M-16 return fire and the distinctive rattle of the Russian AK-47 attack rifles the VC used. Firefight! I could see their muzzle flashes, and the bullets were coming straight at us. It seemed like several minutes passed until I realized that they were shooting at me.

It is the strangest feeling in the world to know there is another human being a few yards away trying with all his might to kill you.

I rolled into some thicker cover and dragged the lieutenant behind me—he was hit. For some reason, I wasn't. It was a typical VC tactic to spring a booby trap, wait until the medic and the ranking officer came up to the front, and then fire away with everything they had. Officers were prime targets, but medics had a twenty-five dollar bounty on their heads, because if you killed the medic all the wounded died. To a Vietnamese peasant who made five dollars a month, that was a lot of money.

Foster, the young second lieutenant, was hit in a bad place, in the midsection and obviously through an organ, probably his kidney or spleen. I did as much as I could, but there was no way I could stop the internal bleeding. Several of our men had been killed outright in the ambush. Bullets zinged and foliage fell as their withering fire kept up. It was getting dark.

I used what was left of my morphine on Brubaker and Foster, until it ran out before midnight. We were pinned down and couldn't escape. Only four of us were alive, but the VC must have thought it was more, because they didn't move in, but just kept our heads down with occasional

A Bahá'í Goes to War   167

bursts. Our radioman was dead, his radio riddled with bullet holes, which meant that we couldn't call in for support in the form of artillery or gunships or anything else.

As soon as the last of the morphine wore off, Foster began to scream. He screamed for his mother, for his girlfriend, for God, for death. The jungle at night is excruciatingly quiet, and his screams pierced the silence and rattled us all. I tried to quiet him, but he wouldn't shut up. We could hear the VC laughing at his terror. We were surrounded, outnumbered and outgunned, out of supplies, in unfamiliar jungle, cut off from our base, and two of the living were wounded. Brubaker could hold a weapon and fire, but not the lieutenant. Washington was whole. I was the crucial third man, and they all knew I was a C.O.

"Whyn't you pick up The Hick's piece and lay down some fire?" Washington asked in a whisper. All three of them knew that their lives rested, at least to some degree, on whether or not I would compromise my principles and start shooting. All kinds of conflicting impulses ran through my mind—'Abdu'l-Bahá's allowance to protect others but not yourself with violence; the conviction that killing someone else, no matter what the circumstances, would be the ultimate betrayal of my beliefs; the strong instinct of self-preservation.

"No can do," I told Washington. If I started shooting once, where would I draw the line?

"Shee-it," he drawled. "I gotta respec' you for that, doc. But we about to git wasted here." As he said it we ducked, because the sound of heavy weapons fire started up again. It was away from us this time, toward the rear of the main VC position. We could hear the bark of an M-60 and several M-16s firing away on full automatic, what the grunts called "rock'n'roll." Then we could hear the VC moving away, the occasional reports of their weapons growing fainter.

A giant smile spread across Washington's face. "The f--king mounties to the rescue," he said happily.

They told us later that it was Foster's screams that had alerted the search party to our location. But before they got there, Foster stopped screaming.

Ralph Purpura came to me one day, while we were on a muddy hilltop firebase called O'Reilly. Ralph was a little guy from Brooklyn, who for some reason took a great deal of perverse pleasure in telling me about the various atrocities that occurred. He'd watch me closely for my reaction, then leave, satisfied that there was somebody he could still disgust.

"Hey, doc, come here, I got somethin' to show ya," he said.

"I'm busy, Ralph."

"No, I'm serious, man, the guy needs help. I think you ought to hurry."

Even though I knew Ralph wasn't the type to go for help, I went.

"It's a new deal—airborne guts," explained Ralph excitedly as we reached another part of the firebase and he showed me the prisoner, tied to a fencepost a hundred yards away. Guts was a Marine invention the Army had adopted, which involved taking a Vietnamese prisoner, tying him or her upright to a stake, then marching by in a line, with every soldier hitting, gouging, kicking, stabbing or otherwise creatively injuring the hapless victim. You were "gutless" if you didn't stand in the line.

Helicopters buzzed overhead, like they always did in Vietnam, but there were several turning circles above us. When they'd get into position, the door gunners would fill the air with flying machine-gun bullets, a visible stream of death pouring down at the small Oriental body strapped to the fence. Even though he was obviously already dead, nothing now but flayed red meat, the body would jump and flinch, making it seem like it was doing a hideously animated dance. Purpura laughed wildly at the look on my face. I turned and walked back.

When people died, as people do in wars, it was not television or movie death. Their deaths were usually quiet, quick, unaccompanied by theatrics or histrionics, final.

One day Greg Stein and I were sitting on a rock eating our Cs. He was talking about his girlfriend and his car, blonde-haired Sarah and a 440 Super Bee, the two seemingly inseparable because he never mentioned one without the other. Then he toppled over on his back, his ham and lima beans spilling everywhere. I looked down. There was a neat, circular hole through his cheekbone. His eyes were open, and he was looking up at me, the life still in him but stealing away, as though he was perturbed at not finishing his thought. Somebody yelled "Sniper!" and everybody hit the dirt. I cradled his head in my hand, but I had forgotten what an AK-47 round is designed to do. When it hits it tumbles end over end through its target, which means the entrance hole is small but the exit hole is a gaping fissure. This is not really ingenious or exclusively diabolical—the American M-16 round does the same thing. Both were designed, no doubt after years of diligent "defense" research and testing, and the expenditure of large amounts of tax money, to do the maximum amount of damage to human tissue. So when he died in the next second, his eyes still open and looking at me, my palm came away holding the back of Greg Stein's skull.

We would occasionally tend to wounded Vietnamese civilians who we came across—the unfortunate, the innocent, the truly noncombatant, who always got the brunt of any war. Children, old people, pregnant women, they were war's most pathetic victims.

We went into a village that had been bombed on what was called a "mop-up" operation. "Suspected communist activity," the captain had said. We found dozens of wounded mothers and children—no men. All were in agony. We treated them as best we could, but for most of them there was no hope, because they had been pierced all over by tiny plastic flechette darts from the American antipersonnel bomb called the "Daisy Cutter." (The name was literal, because it was often used to clear a wide swath of jungle, the thousands of darts levelling every kind of vegetation in a 500-yard circle.)

"Can't we medevac these people to a hospital, Captain?" I was frustrated, mad—furious at my own country.

"Nope," he said. "Those darts won't show up on the X-ray—they're plastic, man. No way to get 'em all out."

"Then these people just have to die slowly?!" I was furious, my jaw muscles clenched, my teeth grinding. "These kinds of weapons are outlawed by the Geneva Convention!" The universal sound of children crying in pain came from the huts.

He scoffed and shook his head at my innocent stupidity, snorting through his nose, and marched us out of the village.

Field medics learn a lot about death in Vietnam, but I learned something I hadn't bargained for.

We were in the middle of another fire fight, this time in the A Shau valley, that stretch of mountainous jungle west of Da Nang in I Corps that every American G.I. feared. Roads, North Vietnamese trucks, tanks, artillery, huge phantom divisions of well-armed, well-trained NVA soldiers that bivouaced in massive underground tunnel systems right underneath your feet—those were the stories about the A Shau. Right next to the Cambodian border, the A Shau contained about a hundred miles of the infamous Ho Chi Minh trail, the conduit for supplies to the guerilla forces in the south. Of supreme military and tactical importance to Vo Nguyen Giap, the North's brilliant military commander and strategist, the Ho Chi Minh trail was protected and maintained by gigantic troop strength numbers. Many American and South Vietmanese forces had gone into the A Shau and come back decimated. The survivors usually returned with the "thousand-yard stare," that unmistakeable vacancy in the eyes of the combat veteran who has looked into the maw of the basest region of man's nature.

This firefight was a running, hot one, the bullets flying and the action fast. Several of our men were down. I tended to the wounded, triaging the most serious as always, and carrying the few who would make it back to the landing zone where the medevac choppers were able to sit down. One man, a young black named Riley, was hopeless, so I made the decision to keep him off the chopper for the first pull, because there were eight others who had much better chances if they got out first. I was making him comfortable as the medevac left, covering his face so the rotor wash wouldn't spray him with dirt and rocks.

"You didn't put me on the firs' flight out, doc," he said weakly, a statement that implied the question he already knew the answer to.

I shook my head at him. Tears came to my eyes. That didn't occur very often, at least not until later when I had time to think about what happened, and I was surprised at myself. It must have shown.

Riley tried to laugh. "Why you cryin', white boy? I'm dyin' an' you cryin'. I *am* goin' to die, right?" I looked at his kinky black hair and his black pockmarked face and at the yellow whites of his brown eyes and saw every other human being at once in his countenance, and it struck me like a mailed fist in the Adam's apple.

"Um-humh," I told him, my throat knotting and my chin trembling. Get a grip, I was telling myself. I barely knew Riley at all.

"You a religious dude," Riley said, faint. "Pray, man."

I said that beautiful prayer from 'Abdu'l-Bahá that starts out *"Oh God, refresh and gladden my spirit..."* I held Riley as I prayed and my chest filled up with remorse and sadness and pain and a bursting, burning feeling of my connection to him, so strong and hard that it made the tears pour from my eyes. They ran down and mingled with the sweat and blood on his jungle fatigues. He died. And there was something, this ineffable lightness, that went away from him, not in any physical sense but in a palpable way that I'll never forget. His body was heavier, leaden, without purpose as it departed. It was then that life after death was confirmed for me, confirmed absolutely.

"Alláh'u'Abhá," I said aloud, like I always did when I was present at the death of another. At that moment—and I hesitate even to commit this to paper because the moment was then so sacred and so basic—my own being lifted inside me and wanted, against my instincts and my will but still unbearably and irresistibly *wanted*, to go too.

Now when I travel to Washington, to the Vietnam Veteran's Memorial, of all the names I know on those black granite slabs, Riley's is the one I search out and stand next to.

We're in our bunkers at Firebase Bastogne near the DMZ, under intense rocket and mortar attack. It is February 13, my twenty-first birthday and the third year since becoming a Bahá'í. Seven months have passed since I arrived in Vietnam.

The rockets cease. Several are injured, but everyone knows that the VC will stop their attack, wait a few minutes for everyone to get up out of the bunkers, then renew it with a few more rockets. So everyone stays down, except Cooper, a chubby, fuzzy-cheeked helicopter pilot who has been drinking all day. He drunkenly stands up and begins to relieve himself on the ground. "Get down, you idiot!" several people yell. Another rocket whistles in, making a terrible ripping noise in the sky like someone tearing enormous sheets of canvas, impacts and explodes directly in front of the standing Cooper. He is killed instantly, blown into small pieces that one other medic and I later police up and put into a body bag. It is not even a quarter full when we are through. The other medic, who carries a big .45 in a holster at his side Western-style, says "Bet this funeral gonna' be closed-casket, hey?" and laughs.

My friend Stewart is wounded. "It's just a nick across the knee," he tells me. "A scratch." We understand each other—both from the West, both like the same music, the same books. I've taught him the Faith, and he is ready to declare. When you literally give someone the responsibility for your very life every day, you tend to get close fast.

"You're going to the evac hospital, anyway," I tell him.

"Not a chance," he says, macho. "A cheap heart." A cheap heart is a Purple Heart, the medal given for sustaining wartime injuries, awarded for a nick or a flesh wound.

"So what?" I ask. "Get on the damn chopper and go." I tell him that infection in the tropics can be as deadly as bullets or rockets. Reluctantly, he agrees.

The company supply clerk comes around the next day and wakes me up. "Dollar for flowers for Cooper's family," he demands. It is customary for the dead man's unit to send the family flowers, a custom I'm uncomfortable with but can't determine why. I give him a dollar.

The next morning he comes again. "Dollar for flowers for Stewart's family," he says.

I can tell I am beginning to lose it, because I no longer cry.

Another mission through the jungle, this time looking for a downed helicopter and its lost crew. It is a race to find them before the VC do.

We lose. When we get there the crew is dead, mutilated and tortured before they were killed. Blood and entrails are everywhere, and several of the men get sick at the sight. The crew's eyeballs have been plucked out, all eight of them lined up on the ground in front of the helicopter, and smashed. "Very bad. Means they can see us, but we cannot see them," says the Vietnamese scout. We glance nervously into the mute jungle around us.

Another time in the A Shau we're caught in an ambush. Fire is coming from all sides, people are screaming and hollering, the noise and the intensity are deafening. We can't move in any direction, so the new lieutenant calls in napalm and artillery so close to our position that it routs the VC, but kills three of our men. "Friendly fire," the Army calls this cause of death.

In the next firefight, the lieutenant is hit. I try to save him. His injury is unusual—he's hit in the back by an M-16 round. He dies.

I see a few of the friends of the three "friendly fire" casualties smiling. "Friendly fire, my ass," one says.

We march into a village in an area where we've been taking sniper fire for days, with five casualties. The platoon's anger level is incredibly high—they've been sitting ducks for the sniper's potshots, but we have nothing to shoot back at but phantoms. "If these yellow bastards'd just come out and fight!" one man growls. Especially galling to them has been the opening of the Army's trial for Lieutenant Rusty Calley, accused of the massacre at My Lai. Also, the platoon comedian, a friendly sort who had plans to become a singer and dancer after the war, is one of the sniper victims, hit in the spine and paralyzed for life.

The village is typical—pigs, water buffalo, chicken, grass huts, rice paddies, women, children, the very old. We search it.

"Hey, doc," Ski the platoon sergeant calls. "Check this out."

He is standing outside a hut and pointing his rifle in. Inside the dark hootch there is a small boy, no more than eleven or twelve, lying on his stomach in obvious pain. Blood stains the rice mat and the ground underneath him. A toothless old woman squats nearby. There is an eerie silence. His eyes are closed, but as I roll him over they open, and I see deep hatred and fear. He is clutching something in his left hand. He looks at me. For a split second time is suspended—he does nothing and I do nothing and we are fixed, rooted there. In the next moment there is gunfire, Ski blasting the kid with a burst on automatic.

"What the hell?!" I jump back. The old crone runs. My face and arms are covered with blood and bits of skin and bone. Ski tips over the kid's limp, demolished body with the tip of his boot. There is a loaded AK underneath.

"Our sniper," he gloats. "Nailed the little f--ker. You gotta be more careful, doc."

"No, Langness," the captain is telling me, "it's policy. No getting around it. Medics in the 101st can't stay in the field for longer than seven months. You've been here eight. You're out—got a rear job. Remington Ranger. Most people're glad to hear that."

"Why?" I asked. "What the hell does a policy like that do? I'm a good medic, and now the company's going to get someone green who doesn't know their ass from an Ace bandage." I was mad again.

"Why? I'll tell you," the captain said. "You're the perfect example, Specialist. Because medics tend to go south on us after that length of time in combat. You know—Looney Tunes. They begin to think they're the only ones can take care of 'their' troopers. They do crazy stuff—like refuse transfers out of the field. Stuff any normal person wouldn't do. Face it, Langness, you and humpin' the boonies are history."

The new job was air traffic control at Camp Eagle, the home base of the 101st near the South China Sea on the eastern coast of South Vietnam. Eagle was a big base, complete with mess halls and an airfield and permanent buildings and a theatre and all the comforts of home, almost. I slept on a bed and had a fan and could usually take a shower (cold), and ate hot meals (lukewarm). My books reposed on a shelf, where I could read them. I had a radio, so I could listen to the absurd disc jockeys on the Army's Armed

Forces Radio Network station play Bob Dylan and Jimi Hendrix and remind us all to take our malaria pills and watch out for booby traps. Then again, we were rocketed often, the base was infested with giant tropical cockroaches and cat-sized wharf rats, the racial tension was so thick it often exploded into violence and death, the heroin epidemic among American soldiers was in full swing, and the air was always putrid with the smell of burning feces, which was the sewage disposal method of choice among those who ran the place.

I'm walking up to the mess hall to eat lunch one day, weak from dysentery. Everyone in the company had suffered from it recently, and the pain was excruciating. All day spent doubled over in an outhouse wishing you would just die and get it over with was the general symptom. No one seemed to be able to figure out where we all got it. General consensus said the mess hall, but the mess sergeant vehemently insisted all his water was pure.

I hear a commotion in the back, go around, and see that the water truck is delivering a load into the mess hall's big tank. The top of the tank is folded back, and the Vietnamese truck driver's two small children are merrily swimming in it for relief from the heat. Four or five men from the company are screaming murderously at the driver, who is screaming back in Vietnamese.

"You dirty son-of-a-bitch, these kids peeing in our water—no wonder the whole damn place's got the shits!"

"I'm going to waste you and these runts!" said another G.I., brandishing his pistol.

"Can't get dysentery from that," I say, lying. I knew immediately that the kids were the cause.

"Doc oughta know," says one, calming down. A few others drop their weapons.

"Bulls--t!" says another. "Who knows what kinda diseases them kids got?"

A Bahá'í Goes to War 177

"Get out of here, papa-san," I say. "Di-di-mau!"

It is tense. The driver is afraid if he moves, the angriest one will shoot.

"Go on, go!" I shout. Kids and dad pile into the truck, and gun it. No one shoots. The water truck careens away.

"Gook-lover," the angry one glowers at me. He has a Confederate flag sewn on his cap.

One day a sergeant and a major come around and collect all the writing paper, pencils and envelopes, bag them, and put them in a big sack.

"No writing home for the next week," they told everybody. They wouldn't answer questions. "You'll get your stuff back later."

But the word got around quickly.

"We're invading Cambodia," everyone said.

On the radio station the disc jockeys read the news of Kent State and the strikes, then played Eric Burdon and the Animals singing "We Gotta Get Outta This Place."

I'm up working at night and the rockets start flying. One-twenty-twos are Russian-made, about the same size as a telephone pole, range twenty-five miles, with enough explosive capability to demolish a good-sized building. They blow up on impact, throwing a broad arc of superheated shrapnel in front of them.

"Incoming!"

I run for the bunker, then remember Eddie and the others, all of them high from smoking heroin, in their hootch. They'll be on the nod. They won't hear. I don't think, and run back toward the shack.

The VC have us bracketed, which means that one rocket has landed too far away in front of us, one too far away in back, and now the on-target ones are landing in the middle. Some hit helicopters, producing a ball of flame and tons of lethal, flying metal. One rocket hits the Officer's Club, smashing it flat. Limp bodies are flung out. Screams fill the silence between blasts. I run.

Their hooch door is locked. I kick it down. The four of them look up at me stupidly. "Incoming, you fools!!" I scream at them, pushing and shoving them out the door. They smile and giggle.

Fires blaze and bodies litter the ground. Illumination flares are up, casting their ghostly white phosphorous light down on us. We run, me prodding them. Eddie falls. More explosions. Smoke clogs my lungs, the pungent smell of cordite and gunpowder fills the black air. I grab Eddie's shirt collar, yank him up, shove him ahead.

We reach a ditch, a crude uncovered bunker. The four of them tumble in. I stand on the edge and look for a place to wedge down amongst the bodies, but it is no use, soldiers jammed together in panic filling the hole. Raw fear banishes even the smell of cordite from my nostrils, washing over me and coming up off the men like fumes from some deadly toxin.

There is another ditch fifty yards away. I run some more, faster than I've ever run before. I can see, out of the corner of my eye, a rocket dopplering in, ripping that sky. It is too close . . . I see I won't make it. Here it comes. All I can do is jump. There are twenty feet left, and I leap. My life really does roll past my open eyes, in slow motion, with everyone in it smiling, happy, alive. I will die. I remember the phrase for great mortal danger from the Kitáb-i Aqdas, and I scream it out. The rocket hits the ground and buries itself. It does not explode—it's a dud. I land on the hard earth and scrape my face and my chest bloody on the rocks, sliding to the edge of the bunker. The feeling of the pain is wonderful.

My own blood is warm and thick, tastes salty in my mouth. I am once again laughing uncontrollably. The boys in the bunker are cheering, laughing, giving me a big hand.

I'm going for a little three-day vacation, called R&R for rest and recovery, at a beach resort named China Beach, near Da Nang. I catch a ride in a helicopter with two Green Berets and a Vietnamese interpreter ferrying two tied-up VC prisoners from Eagle to the main interrogation center at Da Nang. Helicopter rides are nice, because the air at five thousand feet is cool and refreshing, blowing in from the open doors and drying the sweat for once. I'm riding along, looking down at the beautiful lush greenness of Vietnam. Two things strike me from up here—the bombed areas, cratered like the moon, devoid of any sign of life; and a huge peace symbol, dug into the ground by some wag of a G.I. Caterpillar driver, only visible from the air.

Then I turn around and look at the Green Berets, and there is only one prisoner, with an expression of pure terror on his bruised face. The pilots are flying along nonchalantly, oblivious.

One of the Green Berets looks back at me and grins, as does the interpreter. Then I start to understand.

"What the hell happened?!" I yell over the wind noise.

"Huh?"

"Where's the other one?!" I am enraged, bellowing at them.

"Jumped," the grinning one grinned again.

The pilot turned around and winked.

One night, in my final month there, I heard a muffled explosion, close. I ran up the hill toward the rebuilt Officer's Club. It was still standing, but the windows and doors were blown out, and smoke was pouring from them. People stumbled and staggered out, dazed, cut, bleeding from the ears and everywhere else, all of them deaf from the compression shock.

"What happened?" I hollered at them.

They couldn't hear, and kept looking at me quizzically. One finally read my lips.

"Grenade," he said, "the damn militant niggers."

Someone had strapped a grenade under one of the tables in the club, rigged it to go off with movement, and killed sixteen officers, injuring seventy others. The officers (who were predominantly Southern and almost all white) had, just the week before, banned the "black power" handshake, known as the pound; black wristbands and headbands that were worn as a sign of solidarity; and any clenched-fist salute. They had also reassigned some of the base's most visible and articulate black leaders to the field. All this was an attempt to defuse the mounting racial tension among the G.I.s, but it served the opposite end.

The club was smoking less now. I went in, and it was carnage. Bodies were heaped and piled everywhere. The walls literally ran with blood. Groaning and cries for help came from under mounds of the dead. I started pulling at arms and legs wildly. One boot I grabbed came off with a foot still in it. I threw up. Others joined in to help. We lined the bodies up outside and loaded the injured into jeeps and ambulances.

The Army never publicly acknowledged that this incident happened. All of the officers were listed as "Killed in Action." No suspects were ever named.

I was the first medic there, and I spend most of the night working until I thought I would drop from exhaustion. When I dragged myself back, as the sun was rising, I was met by the black corporal who lived next to me, Gordon Haithcock. He saw my bloody arms and sleeves, and asked me what happened.

"Bunch of officers got killed by a grenade in the O club," I said.

"I bet it was those damn redneck bastards," Gordon said angrily, "trying to make the brothers look bad."

On my last night, we were rocketed again. This time I found myself strolling to the bunker, in no hurry. When I got there, it was Haithcock who said, "Doc, you're one crazy mother. Walkin' cool under the incoming, an' so short you could sleep in a matchbox."

I laughed. Haithcock could always make me laugh, with his mischievious eyes and his deadpan expression. We sat down with our backs to the bunker wall. Rockets kept exploding.

"No, I mean it, doc. What is it? Everybody 'round here says you charmed, some kinda good juju, that crap. Man, I'm from Lima, Ohio. I don' believe in juju, any'a that other s--t."

"Gordon," I said, "I don't know. Ever since that dud one-twenty-two I am not, well, ah . . . I don't know how to say it. I'm not—well, death and I seem sort of friendly. That make any sense?"

"No."

"Knew it wouldn't."

"You crazy," he said again. Rockets were still landing, but further away.

"You really want me to explain?"

"F--kin' A," he said.

"Okay. I'm a Bahá'í, you know that."

"Yeah. Says so on your dogs, mus' be oh-ficial. I *am* goin' to look into that like I promised when I get home."

"Good. In the Bahá'í writings, it says that each one of us is like a lamp, an oil lamp, with so much fuel."

"Fatalism," he said. Gordon had the street jive down, but he had seen his share of philosophy in college classes.

"Of a sort."

"Well, hell, that explains it." He leaned back and relaxed.

"What?" I asked, wanting to know how he felt about it.

"Oh—not jus' you crazy, all them Bahá'ís be crazy."

We laughed till long after the rockets stopped.

When I flew out of Camp Eagle for the last time, I looked back down at Vietnam and felt an overwhelming sense of deprivation and loss. All of the death sat on me like a hideous huge buzzard, staring straight into my brain with its red eyes. I resolved to stare back and never forget.

Thirty-six hours away from being rocketed in a foxhole in South Vietnam, I walked into my parents' living room, out of the Army forever. There was a hearty reception at the airport and at home, from my brothers and sisters, but nobody mentioned the war. They did want to know what the medals on my uniform were for. I couldn't wait to get it off and get into civilian clothes.

Being home was one of the strangest feelings I have ever experienced. I was disoriented, like I was walking in some waking dream. So much had changed for me, but little had changed here. It was as if I had been away on an extended vacation. When I walked in the door, the television was on. For some reason, that infuriated me, and for months I could not bear to have a TV on in the same room. It was as if those gifted with life were docilely content to sit and watch artificial life in a box. "No!" I felt like shaking them. "Live!"

Then there was the reunion with all of my Bahá'í friends, who did ask me about the war—what I'd felt, what I thought, how it was. But by that time I didn't want to talk about it, so I was reticent, and would change the subject. I'd told a few people about some of it. The shock of it was so far removed from their experience that I couldn't bear to see the look in their eyes when they realized the gulf that now separated us. So I dodged their kind questions. They could see I didn't want to talk about it, so they stopped asking. Everybody was happy, friendly, welcoming, and that was healing for me. We laughed the most when I took out my prayerbook, the new one they had given me before I left,

and they could all see how tattered and torn it had become.
"Wore that sucker out," Bob chuckled.

After a while, the war receded. Life resumed. There were nightmares, waking up sweating and gasping for air and screaming, but they went away after a few years.

Only one is left, and it recurs occasionally, every six months or so: In it, I'm back in my jungle fatigues, back in Vietnam, and the war is still on. Mortars and rockets and small arms fire are exploding all around the perimeter of the little base we're on. We're about to get overrun by waves of VC sappers. I am calmly trying to talk to the officer in charge, telling him this is all a mistake, I've done my time and been here before, and besides that, all this killing and maiming and grief are for nothing.

He isn't listening.

What About The Russians?

by Brad Pokorny

WHAT ABOUT THE RUSSIANS?
 A simple question, but it stops people cold when thinking about peace and disarmament. No matter how much they hate war, no matter how much they want to eliminate nuclear weapons or establish universal peace, many find this simple question an insurmountable hurdle to imagining any radical change in the West's armament policies.
 Just four words, they raise serious issues for most Americans: How can we make peace with a people whose goals and ideology are so different from ours? How can we trust leaders who seem so evil, who appear so committed to aggression? How can we verify disarmament agreements when the Soviets insist on being so secretive? Isn't the only safe course to play hard and fast on the world scene, showing that we are as tough as they are?
 If we are to establish the just and universal peace that the essays in this book propose, we must first deal with the *Russian* question. For it applies not just to the "Soviet threat," but to the general fear of breaking down barriers of national sovereignty and moving toward the kind of world political organization that must be established if we are to abolish the threat of nuclear annihilation.

Answers to this question do not come easily, nor will they be easily accepted. Throughout the history of the world, variations on the question have stymied peace efforts, helping to color our collective past with blood. Whether it was the Spartans, the Barbarians, the Arabs, or the Germans, fear of outsiders has fueled the rhetoric and the weapons-building that lead to war. The question has been used repeatedly to block efforts at reconciliation and reconstruction.

Bahá'ís believe, however, that humanity has entered a new age. We have at last become mature enough to understand and to call a halt to the cycle of mistrust, fear and hatred that breeds war. Modern transportation and communication systems now make it possible to treat the world as one entity. That, Bahá'ís believe, makes the difference. Since the Bahá'í Faith's turbulent beginnings in the nineteenth century, its followers have consistently supported the idea of collective security, whereby all nations might come together and agree to banish war—whether through a League of Nations, a United Nations, or an as-yet-uncharted Commonwealth of Earth.

In addition to such long-range and, some say, idealistic remedies, the Bahá'í Faith also offers principles and teachings that can be used *now* to help move us away from our current state of dangerous tension between the superpowers toward a more stable world. Ultimately, the Faith promises to show the way to that era of universal peace that all people have so long dreamed of. And to do that, we must first deal with the question: *"What about the Russians?"*

The answers, I believe, come on two levels.

First, the Bahá'í Faith offers a new way of thinking about our enemies that can help us forge a new and much-needed consensus about the way the West deals with the Soviets. Based on a new psychological and theological view of the world, this new attitude offers us a way to calm unfounded fears about the Russian question, and to move toward a more realistic assessment of who and what the Soviets represent. At the same time, the widespread acceptance of these ideas would help to stimulate political leaders in the West to explore new modes of thought and action in pursuing arms control and disarmament.

Second, the Bahá'í Faith offers specific methods and insights which the West's leaders might use immediately to better deal with Soviet leaders, regardless of their larger attitude. Such measures include, but are not limited to:

☐ A clear mandate for improved communications between the leaders of the superpowers as a first step toward constructive negotiations.
☐ The use of the Bahá'í decision-making method, known as *consultation*, at the arms control bargaining table.
☐ A call for cultural, scientific, and tourist exchanges that would aim to break down misunderstanding about the nature of the peoples on both sides of the superpower barrier.

The Real Question. The fundamental change in the West's relationship with the Soviet Union must begin at the grassroots level, focusing on the way each citizen views the Soviet threat. It is there that politicians find a reservoir of ignorance, fear, and mistrust—high-octane emotions that fuel the arms race. In reality, the issue is not: "What about the Russians?" Rather, the question is: "What about evil?"

It matters not whether we ask about Russians or Germans or barbarians. The issue is the trustworthiness of men. It is about hidden motives and secret plans. It is about whether human nature is essentially good or essentially evil. And about whether reason or force, or some other method, provide the best way to push humanity toward the good.

In part, the power the question holds over America hinges on the Christian view of a divided world: good against evil,

God against Satan. Even for those who are not Christian, this strange duality is reinforced every day. Television and movies constantly portray heroes—James Bond, Magnum P. I., Superman—as incorruptible agents of good, ever fighting the despicable agents of evil—whether the KGB, the Mafia, or just the common criminal. The villain, of course, always shows an ultimate disregard for fair play.

This dichotomy has been imposed on U.S.-Soviet relations, both at the popular level and in the highest political councils. In his recent book, *The Nuclear Delusion*, a former American ambassador to Moscow, George Kennan, categorizes two views of the Russian leadership commonly held in this country. Under the first view, Kennan writes, the Soviet leaders appear "as a terrible and forbidding group of men: monsters of sorts . . . lacking in all elements of common humanity—men totally dedicated either to the destruction or to the political undoing and enslavement of this country and its allies. . . . "[1] In other words, they are evil incarnate, and the United States must treat the Soviet Union with that in mind.

The other view, Kennan writes, holds that Soviet leaders are men much like their counterparts in the West. Differences in their behavior stem from their nation's history and their own conditioning. From this view, the aggressive and repressive actions that so threaten the West are explained by seeing Soviet leaders "as a group of quite ordinary men . . . perhaps the most conservative ruling group in the world, markedly advanced in age, approaching the end of their tenure—" Kennan writes. They are men "seldom easy to deal with, who care more about appearances than about reality, who have an unfortunate fixation about secrecy which complicates their external relations in many ways, but who, despite all these handicaps, have good and sound reason, rooted in their own interests, for desiring a peaceful and constructive relationship with the United States."[2]

What About The Russians? 189

Kennan makes it clear he holds the second view. "I see these men as the prisoners of many circumstances: prisoners of their own past and their country's past, prisoners of the antiquated ideology to which their extreme sense of orthodoxy binds them . . . "[3] This picture of Soviet leadership is much different from the vision most Americans hold. And, in many ways, irrespective of historical particulars and individuals, it is a perspective that is supported by a Bahá'í view of human nature.

Although the writings and teachings of the Bahá'í Faith do not disucss the Russians in particular, they have much to say about humanity's nature, substance and purpose. Where the Christian view holds that all people are divided into two camps, the Bahá'í Faith sees all men and women as essentially one. Variations are due to differences in education or capacity.

At the turn of the century, 'Abdu'l-Bahá said:

> . . . *in all religious teachings of the past, the human world has been represented as divided into two parts, one known as the people of the Book of God or the pure tree and the other the people of infidelity and error or the evil tree. The former were considered as belonging to the faithful and the others to the hosts of the irreligious and infidel; one part of humanity the recipients of divine mercy and the other the object of the wrath of their Creator. His Holiness Bahá'u'lláh removed this by proclaiming the oneness of the world of humanity. . . . He has submerged all mankind in the sea of divine generosity. Some are asleep; they need to be awakened. Some are ailing; they need to be healed. Some are immature as children; they need to be trained. But all are recipients of the bounty and bestowals of God.*[4]

In other words, the Bahá'í Faith offers a new view of the world that bears directly on how we think about—and should treat—our "enemies." God is alone the ruler of the universe:

there is no Satan, no dark force. Evil is not an opposite force that must be challenged with aggression. Rather, it is a dark place that needs illumination, a vacuum that needs to be displaced. The weapons for fighting evil are education, compassion, good example, and just deeds—not rhetoric, saber-rattling, or proxy battles in the Third World. No matter how evil the Soviet leadership may be at present, we must begin with the assumption that there can be a change. They are made of the same dust and possess the same desires that we do. They have the same psychological needs and responses, whatever their exterior seems.

The first step for the West, then, is to recognize this and to begin treating the Soviets as potential friends, instead of as intractable enemies. Since much of the old thinking has its roots in theology, it should not be surprising to suggest that a new theology offers our best hope for surmounting this first barrier to reconciliation between the superpowers.

In *Beyond the Cold War*, British historian E. P. Thompson has identified humankind's seemingly innate fear of the outsider as one of the driving forces of the arms race—and indeed of most wars. He calls this "fear of the Other," writing: "The fear or threat of the Other is grounded upon a profound and universal human need. It is intrinsic to human bonding. We cannot define whom 'we' are without also defining 'them'—those who are not 'us.' 'They' need not be perceived as threatening: they may be seen only as different from 'us'—from our family, our community, our nation. But if 'they' are seen as threatening to us, then our own internal bonding will be all the stronger."[5]

The Other has changed throughout our history, Thompson believes, with Rome focusing on the barbarians and, at one time, the English focusing on the French. Today, he writes, this same exclusivity has become a part of superpower relations: " . . . each sees itself as threatened by the Other; yet at the same time this continuing threat has become necessary to provide internal bonding and social discipline within each [side]." If nothing changes to erase this cycle, Thompson believes, it must end in a "terminal war."

Thompson acknowledges the difficulty of turning this situation around. Jokingly, he suggests at one point that perhaps the only way out of the arms race would be to have the planet invaded "by some monsters from outer space, who would at last bond all humanity against an outer Other." In a more serious vein, Thompson says he believes the real solution lies in "a new kind of internal bonding," which takes the form of "a growing commitment, by many thousands, to the imperative of survival and against the ideological or security imperatives of either bloc or their nation-states."[6]

The Oneness of Humanity. The Bahá'í Faith offers precisely the right means for creating that new kind of internal bonding: the concept of the oneness of humanity. It is a principle that could set aside the concept of the Other forever. In the idea that *"the earth is but one country, and mankind its citizens,"*[7] to quote the Founder of the Bahá'í Faith, there lies an entirely new understanding of ourselves and our relationship to others. The concept begins with the idea of universal brotherhood, a notion touted by many good-hearted souls, and currently embraced under the banners of "spaceship earth," or "planetary citizenship." But it goes far beyond that. Rather than regarding world unity as simply a maxim or standard to live by, Bahá'ís hold this vision to be a reality. The only divisions between human beings are those we put there ourselves: they were not established by God or fate. Any division of the world's peoples—whether into blacks and whites, men and women, the East and West, or the godly and godless—is rejected.

In the nuclear age, the fundamental interdependence of the world's peoples is easily dramatized. The simple fact that one person, by pressing the fabled nuclear button, could destroy all civilization on earth is proof of our essential oneness. Yet most people, in their attitudes about nationalism and war, live in a prenuclear world, one in which the peoples and nations of the planet exist in neat separation, like the patchwork borders on a four-color globe.

Our illusion of intrinsic separation is further dispelled by reflecting on past divisions. During World War II, the Germans and the Japanese were considered the inveterate enemies of the allied nations. Oddly, the Russians were our *allies*. Recently, we celebrated the end of World War II and striking photographs of American and Russian soldiers shaking hands, grinning and dancing together as they met at the Elbe River in Germany were displayed. These images should serve to remind us of the way things could be had not the old fear of the Other intervened. Today, the Germans and the Japanese are Western allies, and the Soviets are pariahs.

Perhaps the best case of an old enemy now embraced is China. During the 1950s, they were thought to be as incorrigible as the Soviets by American leaders. The Chinese brand of communism, with its narrow xenophobia and strident anti-capitalist rhetoric, combined with China's huge population base, made that country appear as a long-term menace. Yet, through diplomatic initiatives begun in the 1970s, America and China by the 1980s had opened their doors to trade and cultural exchanges and no longer regarded each other as vile enemies. There is no reason that similar moves toward reconciliation cannot be made with the Soviet Union.

For Bahá'ís, this new understanding of the unity of humankind is an article of faith. Bahá'ís are proving daily that our apparent differences—whether racial, religious, cultural, or ideological—need not cause strife. The three million Bahá'ís on the planet come from every race, religion and nationality. They not only coexist peacefully, they work and make decisions together despite vast differences in background, education, and culture.

In its 1985 peace letter, the Universal House of Justice offers this growing Bahá'í world community as proof that any differences—ideological or otherwise—can be overcome in the quest for peace:

> It is a single social organism, representative of the diversity of the human family, conducting its affairs through a system of commonly accepted consultative principles, and cherishing equally all the great outpourings of divine guidance in human history. Its existence is yet another convincing proof of the practicality of its Founder's vision of a united world, another evidence that humanity can live as one global society, equal to whatever challenges its coming of age may entail. If the Bahá'í experience can contribute in whatever measure to reinforcing hope in the unity of the human race, we are happy to offer it as a model for study.

Faith and Deterrence. We should not be uncomfortable discussing theology and nuclear strategy in the same context. When examined carefuly, it turns out that the West's entire nuclear policy has become a deity of sorts—and a very strange one. Our rationalizations for the manufacture and deployment of nuclear weapons are based on the loosely-defined theory of deterrence. The theory, simply put, argues that the mere possession of nuclear weapons by one nation will *deter* the other nation from aggression—given the immense destructive power of atomic explosives. Because there is currently no defense against a nuclear attack, so the theory goes, neither side will launch a nuclear strike (or stir up much trouble in the world) for fear of a counter-attack.

Yet this theory is based on a number of assumptions, estimations, and gut feelings—or, to use another word, on faith. Rear Admiral Eugene J. Carrol, who once worked on the Navy operations staff that planned for nuclear war, notes that there are three basic assumptions underlying the theory of deterrence: 1) that nuclear forces will always be controlled by rational leaders; 2) that no aggressor will miscalculate the vital interests of a nuclear power; and, 3) that there will be no accidental nuclear events or command, control, communication, or sensor malfunctions which trigger a nuclear response.[8]

"Both sides rely on the *implicit assumption* that [these] three conditions exist today, and will continue without failure in the future," Carroll wrote recently.[9] What is an "implicit assumption" but faith? In relying on nuclear weapons to provide security, we take it on faith that Soviet leaders will always act rationally, whatever other evil motives we ascribe to them. We take it on faith that an insane man will not rise to power and wipe out the world on a whim. Despite the lack of communication and exchange with the Soviet Union, we take it on faith that their leaders will not miscalculate our intentions or our vital interests. And, despite the utter fallibility of our machines (as well as ourselves), we take it on faith that an accidental nuclear war will somehow be prevented.

The theology behind the West's nuclear strategy becomes more perverse when considered in light of the continual increase in weapons. Each side currently possesses enough deliverable nuclear bombs to destroy its superpower adversary many times over, a situation known as *overkill*. This build-up is based on an extension of the deterrence theory which holds that, if a few bombs deter well, more bombs should deter better. Each side has continued to build more and more weapons, seeking some unspecified degree of superiority.

The notion that more nuclear weapons equals more security stems from an outdated military value. When counting regiments, cannons, or jet fighters, more weapons do give a greater chance for victory. America's power of production was an indisputable factor in the Allied victory in World War II. In the nuclear age, however, this thinking no longer rings true. When a single fusion weapon detonated over New York City can kill more Americans than were killed in all of World War II, or a handful of missiles fired at the U.S.S.R. can wipe out more Russians than died in that war, concepts of superiority become a mere illusion, the dangerous relics of an outdated political mindset.

Yet the idea that nuclear weapons—and the more the better—provide security has become deeply ingrained in American culture. Although many polls indicate that most Americans believe both sides possess too many nuclear weapons, the same polls indicate that most Americans would be unwilling to accept significantly lower levels of nuclear weapons unless the Russians did so too. Our leaders, sensing this, stand fast at the arms control bargaining table, leaving little room for compromise. Yet, if nuclear weapons do not in fact create more security, it is clear that people have misplaced their faith. Notes Stanford University arms control specialist Steven Kull: "Psychologists have found that when people face a threat to which they cannot effectively respond, they tend to generate the illusion that there is some meaningful action they can take to reduce that threat. . . . The American public may be hooked on the quick fix of illusory security that arms building provides."[10]

If we are to get rid of nuclear weapons, there is need of a new faith, a new understanding in this age of planetary interdependence, that will replace our outworn notions of security. And once again, it is not illogical to turn to theology to replace the West's shaky belief in the theory of nuclear deterrence and its aberration, overkill. The Bahá'í Faith offers a holistic world view encompassing realms of morality, economics, psychology, theology, and politics. Within those teachings lie that new understanding of what makes for true security. At its foundation that understanding is based on something most people in this country already have: faith in an all-powerful God that cares for us, protects us, and desires the best for us.

All the world's great religions, of course, offer peaceful ideals, teaching that reliance on God is the only real stronghold in this shifting and ever-changing material realm. But that imperative has faded as various sects and interpretations have arisen. Some groups interpret the Bible to support the current build-up of weaponry, while in the Middle East, fanatical followers of religions wage wars in the name of God.

The Bahá'í Faith, however, with its principle of religious unity, lends a fresh impulse to the call for world peace and reliance on God as our only true security. *"The essence of all power is God's, the highest and the last End of all creation . . . ,"* Bahá'u'lláh wrote. *"Such forces as have their origin in this world of dust are, by their very nature, unworthy of consideration."*[11] The Bahá'í concept of progressive revelation further reinforces this reliance. Many people in the modern age have fallen away from a faith in the promises and assistance of God. They have come to look at religion only as a collection of ethical principles and/or a comforting program of therapeutic fellowship and meditation. While they often continue to stand by the faith of their parents, they see little evidence that God continues to shape the affairs of the world, imagining that God confined His interaction with men to biblical times.

The news, as proclaimed in the Bahá'í Faith, that God has continually sent divine messengers to guide humanity provides a revitalizing breath for those who wonder whether God is dead, vacationing, or has otherwise turned His back on this troubled planet. An understanding that His most recent messenger, Bahá'u'lláh, walked the earth less than one hundred years ago and brought a message of peace and unity directed specifically at the needs and issues facing the modern world further helps today's skeptic realize that God does care for us and our world.

In addition to warning against too much dependence on all things material, Bahá'u'lláh specifically warned against an over-reliance on technology, or, to use His term, "civilization." "*The civilization, so often vaunted by the learned exponents of arts and sciences, will, if allowed to overleap the bounds of moderation, bring great evil upon men. . . . The day is approaching when its flame will devour the cities. . . .* "[12]

Moreover, Bahá'u'lláh was unequivocal about the need for disarmament: " . . . *reduce your armaments, that the burden of your expenditures may be lightened, and that your minds and hearts may be tranquillized*," He wrote in a letter to the kings of the earth.[13]

Security, in the Bahá'í view, is not dependent on armies, bombs, or missiles, but on faith in God—and in each other. It is time, Bahá'ís believe, to challenge the notion that human beings are innately violent and aggressive and can only be governed by force. We must open the door instead to a reevaluation of the ideologies and prejudices that divide the world. The Universal House of Justice, in its 1985 peace statement, called for such a reevaluation:

> The time has come when those who preach the dogmas of materialism, whether of the east or the west, whether of capitalism or socialism, must give account of the moral stewardship they have presumed to exercise. Where is the "new world" promised by these ideologies? Where is the international peace to whose ideals they proclaim their devotion? Where are the breakthroughs into new realms of cultural achievement produced by the aggrandizement of this race, of that nation or of a particular class? Why is the vast majority of the world's peoples sinking ever deeper into hunger and wretchedness when wealth on a scale undreamed of by the Pharaohs, the Caesars, or even the imperialist powers of the nineteenth century is at the disposal of the present arbiters of human affairs?
>
> Most particularly, it is in the glorification of material pursuits, at once the progenitor and common feature of all such ideologies, that we find the roots which nourish the

falsehood that human beings are incorrigibly selfish and aggressive. It is here that the ground must be cleared for the building of a new world fit for our descendants.

That materialistic ideals have, in the light of experience, failed to satisfy the needs of mankind calls for an honest acknowledgement that a fresh effort must now be made to find solutions to the agonizing problems of the planet.

Wisdom and Verification. Some readers, at this point, may conclude that Bahá'ís would be willing to retreat and surrender to reach a comprehensive arms control accord with the Soviets, that a Bahá'í-run peace program would mean unilateral disarmament. Far from it. The Bahá'í teachings insist on moderation and practicality in all things. 'Abdu'l-Bahá once said:

> *By a general agreement all the governments of the world must disarm simultaneously and at the same time. It will not do if one lays down the arms and the other refuses to do so. The nations of the world must concur with each other concerning this supremely important subject, thus they may abandon together the deadly weapons of human slaughter. As long as one nation increases her military and naval budget, another nation will be forced into this crazed competition through her natural and supposed interests.*[14]

Yet, in forty years of arms control negotiations between the superpowers, neither side has agreed to dismantle a major weapons system. Treaties that ban nuclear weapons testing in the air, sea, and in space have been signed. Limits have been placed on the deployment of some weapons. But the arms race has not slowed, and the position of each side has only grown more inflexible. There is need for a complete reevaluation of the positions of each superpower as they approach the arms control table. And, once again, the principles of the Bahá'í Faith, I believe, could aid greatly in showing the way to such a reevaluation.

One of the greatest stumbling blocks to arms control, for example, has been the problem of verification: How much can one side take the other's word that the weapons stockpile has been reduced? How does each side verify that arms control limits are being met? In the past, a primary reason given by the United States for the inability to reach a comprehensive arms accord is the reported unwillingness of the Soviets, with their emphasis on internal secrecy, to allow on-site inspections.

Bahá'ís, I believe, would not advocate blind trust on this score. The quality of wisdom, along with compassion, is an essential value.

Nor do Bahá'ís close their eyes to the excesses of the Soviet system. Shoghi Effendi, The Guardian of the Bahá'í Faith, condemned communism specifically, calling it a "false god." He warned that communism, and any other doctrines that "seek to subordinate the sister races of the world to one single race, which discriminate between the black and the white, and which tolerate the dominance of one privileged class over all others—these are the dark, the false, and crooked doctrines for which any man or people who believes in them, or acts upon them, must, sooner or later, incur the wrath and chastisement of God."[15]

In the interim stages of a comprehensive disarmament agreement between the superpowers, it would be foolish for the West not to protect itself by ignoring the need for adequate verification measures. At the same time, however, there is need of a new standard for talk and action as the West tries to win such an agreement—a standard that does not give mixed signals to the Soviets. Our efforts at reconciliation should not be hampered by our distaste for the Soviet System or by our own sense of self-righteousness.

"Shut your eyes to estrangement," wrote Bahá'u'lláh, *"then fix your gaze upon unity. Cleave tenaciously unto that which*

will lead to the wellbeing and tranquillity of all mankind. This span of earth is but one homeland and one habitation. It behooveth you to abandon vainglory which causeth alienation and to set your hearts on whatever will ensure harmony."[16]

Understanding that the earth is but one homeland, regardless of how political leaders divide it, offers a strategy for using technology to assist in overcoming the mistrust that divides the world. Recently, much has been made about the possibility of using space-based weapons to provide an impenetrable shield against intercontinental missles—a sort of strategic end-run to overcome the glaring deficiencies of the deterrence theory. To my mind, however, such an effort only furthers the sense of a divided world, and is therefore spiritually wrong.

Technology could be used, however, to set up a space-based verification system, operated by a third party (such as the United Nations) that would allow the world to rest more easily about troop movements, missile deployments, and weapon testing. Bahá'ís are not against the use of technology, just an over-reliance on it. "*Such arts and sciences, however, as are productive of good results . . . and are conducive to the well-being and tranquility of men have been, and will remain, acceptable before God,*" Bahá'u'lláh writes.[17] Numerous scientists and arms control specialists now say we have the undoubted ability, through surveillance satellites and seismic detectors, to verify whether or not most types of arms control agreements are being kept. For those who somehow feel current technology is not sufficient, there seems little doubt that a crash program of development would succeed in producing reliable equipment to detect any weapons testing in the world. Would it not be better, instead of spending vast sums to place new weapons systems in space, to spend that time and money on a harmless but psychologically effective space-based verification system that could help all the world's peoples feel confident that arms control pacts are kept?

The United States might become the principle creator of such a system. But, in time, it would probably be more effective to have it operated by an independent monitoring agency that acts in the interests of all the nations. It could be operated by the United Nations or, perhaps, by a small, independent group of third party nations that are chosen by both superpowers. These nations, given that even small nuclear exchanges could bring about the destruction of most life on the planet, have as much interest as anyone in insuring that both superpowers hold to arms control agreements.

Such an idea has already been proposed. The development of an International Satellite Monitoring Agency has been discussed for some years at the United Nations. But, as might be expected, the reaction of the superpowers to a possible breach of their monopoly on satellite-gathered intelligence has been less than enthusiastic. There are virtually no technical problems to block the development of such a system; the obstacles are political.

Here again, I believe, it is only by a sweeping change in the average man's view of himself, his nation, and the world that the political impetus for such a proposal will come. An understanding that the earth is one homeland is critical to such a venture. While many organizations now embrace this principle, only the Bahá'í Faith offers the kind of holistic world view that is likely to sway diehard nationalists to this new understanding.

The interim goal for disarmament, to be accompanied by a growing movement for reform and the proper use of technology, would be a level of minimum deterrence—a state where each side has just enough nuclear weapons, mounted aboard stable, relatively invulnerable delivery systems, to deter aggression but not so many that the other side might be fearful of a preemptive strike or other threatening scenarios. In the late-1800s, Bahá'u'lláh admonished nations to possess no armaments *"except for the purpose of preserving the security of their realms and of maintaining internal order within their territories.*"¹⁸ Given the current level of mistrust between the United States and the Soviet Union, such a minimum level of armament is at least a step toward that mandate. Ultimately, combined with a third-party system to verify that minimum levels of weapons are kept, we can assume that a new atmosphere of trust and goodwill would begin to grow between the superpowers. And, from that base, moves toward the long-sought general and complete disarmament could be made.

Concrete Applications. Most of the foregoing has been aimed at outlining how the principles and teachings of the Bahá'í Faith can assist in forging a broad mandate, at the grassroots level, to answer the Russian question—answers that must come if peace is to be established. However, the principles and teachings of the Bahá'í Faith could make an immediate impact at the higher levels of political decision-making and international relations, even if those leaders do not fully subscribe to the new world view outlined here.

This author does not pretend to be an expert on the Soviet Union. So many issues of national security exist in a cloud of seemingly irreconcilable opinions. There are plenty of experts, but few facts or answers. As Kennan noted, there is a basic disagreement over whether the Soviets are power-hungry miscreants or simply paranoid nationalists. However, by stepping back and reevaluating these opinions against the new age teachings and principles of the Bahá'í Faith, we may find a way out of our current dilemma. Bahá'u'lláh promises: " . . . *every matter related to state affairs which ye raise for discussion falls under the shadow of one of the words sent down from the heaven of His glorious and exalted utterance.*"¹⁹

That said, I will suggest specific applications of Bahá'í teachings and methods to our current situation. The first step must come in the area of improved communication between the superpowers. On a broad front, leaders of the

United States and the Soviet Union must begin to speak directly with one another, despite their differences and disagreements. This does not mean just an annual summit or a few letters and phone calls. It means sitting down and making a full exchange of views. Throughout the Bahá'í writings, political leaders are urged to sit down and work out their differences at the conference table, not on the battlefield. *"O ye elected representatives of the people in every land!"* Bahá'u'lláh wrote. *"Take ye counsel together, and let your concern be only for that which profiteth mankind, and bettereth the condition thereof..."*[20]

Many nuclear strategists believe the greatest likelihood for nuclear war comes not from deliberate action, but rather from miscalculation or miscommunication. Political leaders should consider the mandate to *"take counsel together"* as their foremost task, putting it ahead of all other issues on their agenda.

Second, the Bahá'í method of consultation might be applied directly to this stepped-up negotiating process. It is here, perhaps, that the application of Bahá'í teachings could bear fruit most quickly. The method might first be used in the inner circles of power, as leaders seek to define and set policy for a renewed approach to arms control. It could also be used among leaders of Western nations. And finally, it could be applied directly to the negotiating process between the superpowers.

Unlike most decision-making processes, which rely on adversarial fact-finding and analysis, predetermined ideological positions and political compromise aimed at pleasing constituencies instead of solving problems, Bahá'í consultation seeks to discover facts and relationships—regardless of whether they fit into a preconceived framework—and to evaluate those facts against the highest possible standard: what is the best for *all* concerned.

'Abdu'l-Bahá has explained the bedrock rule for participants in the consultative process: *"They must in every matter search out the truth and not insist upon their own opinion, for stubbornness and persistence in one's views will lead ultimately to discord and wrangling and the truth will remain hidden.*"[21] If the world's political leaders are sincere about reaching arms control accords, their first duty must be to step outside themselves and their points of view, and begin to look at the problem from the outside.

This call for new kinds of negotiating and fact-finding techniques is not unique to the Bahá'í Faith. The Harvard Negotiation Project, for example, has developed certain guidelines for effective negotiating that parallel many of the principles of Bahá'í consultation. In *Getting To Yes*, Roger Fisher and William Ury of the Harvard project define a four step method for breaking through traditional negotiating deadlocks: 1) separating people from the problem; 2) focusing on interests, not positions; 3) generating a wide variety of possibilities before deciding what to do; and 4) insisting on some objective standard.[22]

Bahá'í consultation, which predates the Harvard project, employs similar steps. Of primary importance, for example, is the separation or detachment of individual egos and personal agendas from the consultation process. This is accomplished by methods that are both practical and spiritual. Second, by definition, Bahá'í consultation aims at a solution that benefits the widest possible group, whether that be a small village or the whole planet. Predetermined positions are rejected. Third, consultation employs a fact-finding phase that attempts to research all possibilities, no matter how untried or unprecedented, before arriving at a solution. And, fourth, given the Faith's emphasis on science and logic, consultation always strives to base decisions on objective principles.

There is much more to Bahá'í consultation than outlined here. Limited by space, I have tried to show how it parallels the *Getting To Yes* process only for the sake of expediency. There are other principles involved, and they can be listed in any order. In many ways, Bahá'í consultation is an evolving art. There is no established manual or process. Yet, because the Faith provides a new way of looking at the world, and the process of consultation is based on that new understanding, it provides a flexible and effective tool for consensus-building. It is being used with ever-increasing success by diverse groups of Bahá'ís. It provides a sorely-needed alternative to traditional, adversarial, decision-making techniques that have left the world's political leaders in a deadlock.

In its peace letter, the Universal House of Justice has stressed the importance of consultation in the search for peace:

> The intolerable conditions pervading society bespeak a common failure of all, a circumstance which tends to incite rather than relieve the entrenchment on every side. Clearly, a common remedial effort is urgently required. It is primarily a matter of attitude. Will humanity continue in its waywardness, holding to outworn concepts and unworkable assumptions? Or will its leaders, regardless of ideology, step forth and, with a resolute will, consult together in a united search for appropriate solutions?

The third concrete application of Bahá'í principles to our current dilemma, I believe, comes in the call for a new level of cultural, scientific and tourist exchanges. The Universal House of Justice notes: "Current international activities in various fields which nurture mutual affection and a sense of solidarity among peoples need greatly to be increased." Such exchanges are necessary to break down the stereotypes each side holds about the other, and to facilitate the kind of truth-seeking outlined above. Bahá'í pioneers, by leaving their own countries and resettling in other lands, have long striven to break down the old barriers of fear and suspicion, believing that the mere act of acquainting ourselves with other cultures (and of acquainting other cultures with those from outside) serves the ultimate cause of peace.

Increased contact between the peoples of the Soviet Union and the United States can only serve the cause of truth. Each individual who meets someone from the other side will be better able to judge for himself whether the theories of intrinsic separation are true or false, whether the other side is populated with monsters or humans.

What About the Russians? Is there, then, a scenario by which we might see legitimate progress toward arms control and, ultimately, total disarmament, with the Soviet Union without compromising the West's legitimate security interests? And, can the Bahá'í Faith play a key role in guiding us through this process? As outlined above, the Bahá'í principles provide a psychological foundation and a divine standard, against which the West can measure its actions. Given the proper promotion of these principles, and a growing awareness of their importance, we can summarize the following course.

First, armed with a better understanding of what true security is, the West would be better equipped to strike a balance between the type of weaponry it needs to prevent a Soviet attack and the need to reduce the chance of stirring Soviet paranoia and/or setting off World War III through mechanical error or political miscalculation. And, as time passes, the West might gradually become more willing to trade off the unnecessary degree of overkill—which is based on false doctrines and on illusions about what security is—as a means of seeking similar and verifiable arms reductions from the Soviets.

Second, instead of opening up a new battleground in outer space, we could expect the West to divert its technological resources into the more realistic and spiritually-minded task of building a space-based verification network. This will both protect the West (and the World) from subterfuge in the

What About The Russians? 207

arms control process, and help to prove the West's good intentions to the Soviets. Such a program might require greater diplomatic efforts than merely erecting a space-based shield, but that is surely more in line with the spiritual principles taught by all faiths, demanding reconciliation instead of isolation.

Third, once the West has truly adopted a consistent and nonaggressive strategic posture, we can expect, I think, an effect on the Soviet propaganda campaign directed at the Russian people. As things are now, there is enough dissonance between the West's peace-making rhetoric and its war-making capacity to unsettle the hearts of the East's peoples, especially when reinforced with Communist propaganda. But if the West's actions are more clearly aimed at *just* concessions, that message will, sooner or later, filter into the consciousness of the East-block peoples. Whether this message is spread by external radio broadcasts (like the Voice of America) or by underground literature, or simply by word-of-mouth that must come from increased tourist, cultural and scientific exchanges, the change of heart in the West will surely make its example known in the East. And as the bond between the peoples of the two cultures grow, the leaders will find that their power to stir up hatred and fear will diminish.

In addition, we can discern clear signs that the existing order inside Russia is ripe for change—a ripeness that could advance the cause of peace. First, it is inevitable that the membership of the Soviet ruling body, the Politburo, will change dramatically over the next few years, simply because many of its members are so old. The rise of the new Soviet premier, who is among the youngest of the Politburo members, reflects this. Many in the West are hoping he will be more flexible and world-minded than previous Soviet leaders. There will be more changes to come, as other members of the old guard die. An enlightened policy by the West can take advantage of this. Kennan noted: " . . . Soon there will have to be extensive changes in the occupancy of the senior political positions in Moscow, and Western policy makers should consider that a Western policy that offers no encouragement to the more moderate elements in the Soviet hierarchy must inevitably strengthen the hand, and the political position, of those who are not moderate at all."[23]

The ever-worsening economy of the Soviet Union heralds a second opportunity for change. Recent reports tell us of low productivity, shoddy workmanship, and poor worker morale. Just as China has recently turned toward free market ideals to spur its flagging economic growth, so there are indications that Soviet economists are opening the door to new ideas. The deputy chairman of the Soviet state planning agency recently told American journalists that Soviet leaders are considering bonuses and limited profit-sharing plans for efficient workers, along with greater freedom for managers to make production and investment decisions.[24]

Rather than trying to shut down the Soviet economy through trade restrictions or, as some hawkish elements have suggested, force Russia into an all-out arms race that would further distress its economy, the West could encourage the Soviets to venture into the world marketplace. The more the Soviet economy is dependent on outside forces, the more their political leaders will be forced to pay attention to world opinion in areas of human rights and arms control. The Soviet leaders, wrote New York Times economic writer Leonard Silk in 1983, "know they must improve their economy by some measure of liberalization, and they know they need greater trade, especially in technology with the West. If we are ready to bargain with them, they will bargain too, whether on arms or food or energy or gas compressors or pipeline gear—or even on human rights."[25]

The third hope for change inside the Soviet Union rests on what has been a constant theme of this essay: the question of faith. There are numerous signs of spiritual malaise in the Soviet Union. Consider, as evidence, the growing alcoholism and divorce rates there. And, according to some observers, the years of church repression in the Soviet Union have not diminished the spiritual hunger of its people. New York Times journalist David K. Shipler, who spent three years as a Moscow correspondent, believes there is a growing realization among Soviet citizens that communism has not delivered on all of its promises. " . . . In the drifting vacuum left by failing communism, the church holds potential power—not institutionally, but spiritually."[26] Each of these arenas—political, economic and spiritual—provide a window of opportunity for improving the West's relationship with the Soviet Union—or, if the proper initiatives are not taken, for a continued worsening of superpower relations. In the broadest sense, whether the West takes the initiative depends on how it views the Soviet Union: as potential friend or eternal enemy.

Of course, the above proposals for improving East-West relations are not unique. Numerous peace thinkers, diplomats and former military leaders have called for similar steps to slow the arms race: a return to minimal deterrence; a call for greater communication; the rejection of inflexible bargaining positions; etc. The message of Bahá'í Faith, however, holds potential for allowing the peoples of the world to overcome their unfounded fears of the Other at the grassroots level. In forty years of peace promises, the world's politicians have failed to bring about peace. Instead, they have divided their peoples by exploiting fear of the outsider, usually for their own political advantage. The new consciousness, encouraged by the revolutionizing standards and overall context of the Bahá'í Faith, could banish that fear forever, clearing the way for the bold steps that are necessary for reconciliation, reconstruction and ultimate disarmament.

If the West takes any or all of the initiatives proposed above, or if it takes to heart the spiritual principles of the Bahá'í Faith, and the Soviet Union fails to respond with acceptable concessions and proves intractable, nothing will have been lost. The situation will remain the same: with both sides poised in a nuclear standoff, uncertain whether tomorrow will bring some accident or evil design that will trigger the deadly arsenals.

Writing toward the end of the last century, the Founder of the Bahá'í Faith promised that even the hardest heart can be softened, and asked that we fight tyrants with compassion and unity. *"The thick clouds of tyranny have darkened the face of the earth, and enveloped its peoples,"* Bahá'u'lláh wrote, almost as if describing the situation today. He then refers to the new age of human maturity: *"Through the movement of Our Pen of glory We have, at the bidding of the omnipotent Ordainer, breathed a new life into every human frame, and instilled into every word a fresh potency. All created things proclaim the evidences of this world-wide regeneration."*

"Who is it that can dismay you?" Bahá'u'lláh asks, as if responding to the question raised in this essay. *"A touch of moisture sufficeth to dissolve the hardened clay out of which this perverse generation is molded. The mere act of your gathering together is enough to scatter the forces of these vain and worthless people."*[27]

The responsibility for change lies with the West. Only its citizens have the freedom to discuss and act on the kind of compromises that, like a touch of moisture, could begin to dissolve the hard clay that has enshrined the deity of nuclear strategy on both sides—a deity that has become sacred among certain elements in the two superpowers, and one which threatens to destroy them both.

Notes

1. George Kennan, *The Nuclear Delusion—Soviet-American Relations in the Atomic Age* (New York: Pantheon Books, 1983) p. 64.
2. Ibid., pp. 64–65.
3. Ibid., p. 153.

4. *Bahá'í World Faith*, (Wilmette, Ill.: Bahá'í Publishing Trust, 1943) p. 246.
5. E. P. Thompson, *Beyond the Cold War—A New Approach to the Arms Race and Nuclear Annihilation* (New York: Pantheon Books, 1982) p. 170.
6. Ibid., p. 176. I find this "joke" about outer space men more real than imagined. From a Bahá'í point of view, the coming of Bahá'u'lláh does indeed represent intervention by an outside force or being. Only rather than bonding humanity together against a common threat, the potential is for bonding humanity together in recognition of Bahá'u'lláh's divine origin.
7. Bahá'u'lláh, *Gleanings from the Writings of Bahá'u'lláh* (Wilmette, Ill.: Bahá'í Publishing Trust, 1939) p. 250.
8. Gwyn Prins, ed., *The Nuclear Crisis Reader* (New York: Vintage Books, 1984) p. 5.
9. Ibid. Emphasis added.
10. Steven Kull, "Nuclear Nonsense," *Foreign Policy*, No. 58 (Spring 1985) p. 51.
11. *Gleanings* p. 341.
12. Ibid., p. 342.
13. Ibid., p. 250.
14. Quoted in *Waging Peace* (Los Angeles: Kalimát Press, 1985) p. 68–69.
15. Shoghi Effendi, *The Promised Day Is Come* (Wilmette, Ill.: Bahá'í Publishing Committee, 1941) p. 118.
16. *Tablets of Bahá'u'lláh* (Haifa: Bahá'í World Centre, 1978) p. 67.
17. Bahá'u'lláh, *Epistle to the Son of the Wolf* (Wilmette, Ill.: Bahá'í Publishing Trust, 1941) p. 19.
18. *Gleanings*, p. 249.
19. *Tablets*, p. 151.
20. *Gleanings*, p. 254.
21. Quoted in *Principles of Bahá'í Administration: A Compilation* (London: Bahá'í Publishing Trust, 1950) p. 43.
22. Roger Fisher and William Ury, *Getting To Yes: Negotiating Agreement Without Giving In* (Middlesex, England: Penguin Books, 1983) p. 11.
23. Kennan, *Delusion*, p. 155. Can we not also observe a spiritual truth at work here: that this world is subject to constant

change, and we must all face death, as Bahá'u'lláh says in *The Hidden Words*. No matter how great our temporal power, we all remain under the shadow of God.

24. David Ignatius, "Soviet Official Calls for Worker Bonuses, Limited Profit Sharing to Spur Economy," *The Wall Street Journal* (26 April 1985) p. 33.

25. Leonard Silk, "Andropov's Economic Dilemma," *The New York Times Magazine* (9 October 1983) p. 101.

26. David K. Shipler, "Russia: A People Without Heroes," *The New York Times Magazine* (16 October 1983) p. 38.

27. *Gleanings*, p. 92–93.

Biographical Notes

KARIN RYAN BARNES is a Bahá'í living in the Los Angeles area. She is one of the founders of Youth for World Peace.

SUSAN B. BRILL, M.A., M.B.A., is a doctoral student in English literature at the University of New Mexico. Her primary areas of interest are feminist literary criticism, hermeneutics, and nineteenth-century British literature. A former marathon runner, she now balances her intellectual pursuits with competitive bodybuilding.

RICHARD B. HOLLINGER, M.A., is pursuing a Ph.D. in history at the University of California, Los Angeles. He is writing a book on the early history of the Bahá'í Faith in America.

DAVID LANGNESS, M.A., is a writer, journalist, and longtime peace activist. He recently completed his first novel, *Brutal Customs*, and is now at work on a book of interviews with major contemporary American authors.

ANTHONY A. LEE, M.A., C. Phil., is one of the owners of Kalimát Press and acts as its Managing Editor. He is pursuing a doctorate in history at the University of California, Los Angeles.

Biographical Notes

CHARLES O. LERCHE, Ph.D., is a political scientist and a professor in the overseas programs of Boston University, Berlin. He is the editor of a forthcoming volume of essays on world order in the light of Bahá'í teachings.

ROBERT T. PHILLIPS, M.A., C. Phil., owns Consultant Services, a medical management consulting firm. His experience includes positions with the American Lung Association and the University of California.

BRADLEY D. POKORNY is a journalist who works for *The Boston Globe*. He is writing a book on the Bahá'í Faith and peace issues.

ROUHA ROSE holds a M.S.W. from the University of Washington. She has a small marriage counseling practice and is involved in work for the peace movement in the Seattle area.

TAHMINEH ROSHANIAN is a law student at University of California, Hastings. She plans to specialize in International Law and human rights issues.